The Mosque Conflict in Catalonia

The Mosque Conflict in Catalonia

Space, Culture, and Capitalism

Martin Lundsteen

LEXINGTON BOOKS
Lanham • Boulder • New York • London

Published by Lexington Books
An imprint of The Rowman & Littlefield Publishing Group, Inc.
4501 Forbes Boulevard, Suite 200, Lanham, Maryland 20706
www.rowman.com

86-90 Paul Street, London, EC2A 4NE

British Library Cataloguing in Publication Information Available

Library of Congress Cataloging-in-Publication Data

Names: Lundsteen, Martin, 1983- author.
 Title: The mosque conflict in Catalonia : space, culture, and capitalism /
  Martin Lundsteen.
 Description: Lanham : Lexington Books, 2022. | Includes bibliographical
  references and index. | Summary: "In this book, Martin Lundsteen
  investigates the often overlooked political-economic aspects of mosque
  conflicts. Focusing on the mosque project in Barcelona, Lundsteen takes
  a socio-spatial approach, investigating both the local and global
  processes of contemporary capitalism"-- Provided by publisher.
 Identifiers: LCCN 2022029765 (print) | LCCN 2022029766 (ebook) | ISBN
  9781666908954 (cloth) | ISBN 9781666908978 (paper) | ISBN
  9781666908961 (ebook)
 Subjects: LCSH: Mosques--Spain--Premiá de Mar--Organization and
  administration. | Mosques--Social aspects--Spain--Premiá de Mar. |
  Capitalism--Spain--Premiá de Mar. | Premiá de Mar (Spain)--Politics
  and government.
 Classification: LCC BP187.65.S63 P745 2022 (print) | LCC BP187.65.S63
  (ebook) | DDC 297.3/5467--dc23/eng/20220720
 LC record available at https://lccn.loc.gov/2022029765
 LC ebook record available at https://lccn.loc.gov/2022029766

Contents

List of Figures and Tables

Acknowledgments

In the immense multitude of people who have been part of the process of carrying out research for and writing up this book since 2009 (!), I would like to give a special shout out to my partner-in-life Vanessa, my family in Denmark and in Castelló, and all my friends in Barcelona, Castelló, Oxford, London, and Denmark, or wherever you are around these days. The emotional support throughout the years has been the fundament on which a book like this has been able to develop accordingly.

Likewise, I would like to thank all the people who helped me with the research, in the town in Premià, especially Àngel and Joan, or through supervision, Jaume, Susana, Manuel, and Alberto. Your help has been vital. The book would have been completely different or simply would not have been at all. That being said, any incorrection or error is of course *mea culpa*.

Finally, I would also like to give thanks to all the people with whom I have been able to debate, dissent, speculate, and collaborate in terms of research and activism. I think especially of such lucid and rich surroundings as OACU, GER, and SAFI, which have helped me grow both academically and politically-ethically.

Introduction

Of the many conflicts surrounding Muslim places of worship, be they mosques or oratories, which have taken place in Catalonia and Spain at large, the first to make an impact was that of Premià de Mar (Barcelona) in the period 1997–2003. Although there had already been several conflicts in Granada, 1981 (Rosón 2005), and Vic, 1990 (Moreras 2009), none of these had drawn as much attention from the media. The conflict over the plan to construct a purpose-built mosque in Premià de Mar, a small town on the coast of Maresme only thirty kilometers from Barcelona, attracted a great deal of media and political attention, to the point that it became an iconic case, filling plenty of front pages and column inches in the papers and generating many reports both by the public administration and NGOs. Speculation about the event's significant impact abounds and much could be addressed in assessing those arguments, which probably had to do with the specific historical moment in which it occurred (after all, the most extreme events took place between the years 2001–2002, the time immediately following the 9/11 attacks in New York); however, this book will mainly focus on the underlying and inherent structures and dynamics of the conflict at the local level. In any case, because the case was paradigmatic and the first to transcend the locale, because of the precedents to which it gave rise, it is indeed an optimal case to reflect upon the literature on mosque conflicts and the gaps therein.

MOSQUE CONFLICTS: BEYOND IDEOLOGICAL AND CULTURAL CONFLICTS

Many studies have dealt with the rejection of Muslim places of worship worldwide. In 2005, the *Journal of Ethnic and Migration Studies* published a special issue on mosque conflicts in Europe. The vast majority of these conflicts had arisen over the preceding twenty years. Case studies were drawn from different countries, such as the Netherlands (Landman and Wessels

2005), Germany (Jonker 2005), France (Galembert 2005; Cesari 2005), Belgium (Manço and Kanmaz 2005), England (Gale 2005; McLoughlin 2005), and Italy (Saint-Blancat and Schmidt di Friedberg 2005), showing that the phenomenon was indeed general to EU member states. The majority of these scientific articles dealt with cases of rejection. Moreover, even though each case had its peculiarities, the special issue showed how, in general terms, the arguments behind the rejections were very similar to those in the case of Premià de Mar: there is a concern about the central location of the mosque, about the supposed problems of parking and human crowding that it would lead to, a supposed fall in house prices in the area, and later, fear of a future congregation of Muslims in the neighborhood, which is called a "ghettoization." Furthermore, the arguments presented are all based on a perception of the Muslim community as homogeneous, segregationist, and a danger or in opposition to "the community." At first glance it seemed to confirm the hypothesis set out by other authors pointing to a growing Islamophobia at the European level (Cesari 2006), including some of the defects of the most dominant theories, such as the fixation on cultural and symbolic aspects and innocence regarding its material and historical embedding (Müller-Uri and Opratko 2016), and a tendency to treat the phenomenon merely at a psychological and *sui generis* level (Kundnani 2016). Consequently, the approach adopted in the current analysis will offer an alternative reading, complemented with a final reflection on the relationship between Islamophobia and capitalism.

Before this, if we direct our attention to Spain, mainly to Catalonia, where most contemporary Muslim immigration to Spain has concentrated, we see that conflicts around Muslim places of worship began to arise at the beginning of the 1990s. The first known case was in Granada in 1981 when a Muslim association bought land higher up the hill in the Albayzín neighborhood to build a mosque.[1] A neighborhood association prevented the project from taking place until, in 2003, the *adhan* (the call to *salat*–Islamic prayer) was heard for the first time (Rosón 2005). Since then and until the case of Premià de Mar (assuming that it started in 1997), in Catalonia, there have been three more cases: 1990 in Vic (Osona), 1995 in Canet de Mar (Maresme), and 1996 in Roses (Alt Empordà). These cases did not have a great deal of attention or media impact.

Despite the lack of media attention bringing the conflicts into the public eye, there was a new conflict every year from 1995–2000, after which there began a significant increase (Moreras 2009, 50). Moreras makes a crucial point: the first increase was consistent with an increase in the number of faithful Muslims due to family reunification. It is, in fact, at the end of this period when "the first expressed rejection samples appear more intensively" (Moreras 2009, 50). Among the best-known cases in Spain, apart from

Granada, took place in Reus (2000), Santa Coloma de Gramenet (2004),[2] Badalona (2004), Seville (2004),[3] and Alacant (2005).[4]

Looking at the aforementioned cases in relation to the Premià de Mar case, we can make some observations. The first is, as some authors have pointed out (Astor 2009; Moreras 2009), that a significant number of conflicts have taken place in Catalonia, indeed many more than in other autonomous communities. Specifically, in Catalonia there have been forty cases, along with four in Andalusia and six in the Valencian Community, but none documented in Madrid (Moreras 2009, 52). The second is that most of the cases in Catalonia have arisen in neighborhoods with residents from other parts of Spain; working-class neighborhoods where social services and community facilities are often lacking (Astor 2009, 18).[5] The third is that, Premià de Mar as a town presents many of the same social and spatial characteristics observed on the whole (Astor 2009, 27) in neighborhoods throughout the metropolitan area of Barcelona where similar conflicts have taken place. Namely, segregation divides the cities in two: a part where former immigrants from southern Spain predominate (now together with immigrants from elsewhere) and another part where "Catalans" are the predominant group. A fourth observation is that much like many conflicts around Europe these have taken place in the early twenty-first century, although it is true that in France there were many conflicts at least from the 1980s.

Now, if we consider these four observations in relation to the arguments presented during the conflict in Premià de Mar, and also combine them with the specificities of the Lodi case in Italy (Saint-Blancat and Schmidt di Friedberg 2005) which is more similar to this in context, we can distill three elements to consider when analyzing conflicts over the construction of mosques: 1) migration, 2) urban transformation, and 3) political culturalization. These elements can be further distilled into two axes that make up the object of this study: 1) migration and the concomitant transformation of the town and 2) "cultural conflicts."

CULTURAL CONFLICTS

Most of the narratives and interpretations made about the Premià de Mar conflict follow a culturalist reasoning scheme. In other words, according to these, conflicts are essentially intercultural or conflicts that come through different cultures attempting to integrate. Thus, they are based on a particular idea of what culture means and how it influences social relations, which I call primordialist, as opposed to other views such as the dialectical or materialistic views that understand culture as a phenomenon determined by other factors, whether of a political or economic nature, respectively.

Newspaper articles chronicling the event repeat the recurrent argument made in opposition to constructing new mosques, namely the project in Premià de Mar would cause the arrival of an untold number of immigrants from the entire region that would mean "a massive establishment of Muslim families" with the subsequent 'creation of neighborhoods where future *convivencia* will be very difficult' (Pérez 2001).[6] In the words Dídac, member of the neighborhood association of Casc Antic at the time of the fieldwork:

> People have a historical atavism. These people are different. They are strange, they are . . . and of course, and they reject them, because of the way they act around women and such, is a disgusting way, you know . . . And they do not want them there, but you will see that there is not, you don't have such a problem with other communities, such as the Buddhists or the Jews for instance. There's no problem! So ask yourself why . . . Therefore, the rejection of the mosque is because the mosque would mean that, let's say, a certain way of . . . that they are going to congregate there, right? And then, of course, they are going to degrade the neighborhood, because they have a way of living, a way of being, which is totally different from ours.[7]

This idea that the opposition against the construction of a mosque in Premià was a problem of cultural *convivencia* or just a cultural conflict was widespread even among many of the people in favor of the construction. In other words, both sides were convinced that the conflict was of a cultural nature, a problem of *convivencia* between people with different ways of living and customs.[8] This interpretation was accepted so readily, that it crossed the usually contrasting ideologies and social positions of the different actors involved in the conflict, whether they were the town council, the NGOs or the inhabitants of Premià de Mar. That is why we have identified it as the dominant, hegemonic interpretation, since, however they framed it, the majority spoke of cultural *convivencia*, although, of course, there were also people whose perception of things was somewhat critical of this hegemonic vision.

Although the construction of a mosque contains a crucial spatial element, no one talks about space. In addition, although the migrants are primarily workers in agriculture, the construction sector, garages, and domestic services, the majority of studies and the interpretations made both at the street level, as well as by NGOs and the public administration, ignore this fact. On the contrary: the vast majority focus mainly or solely on the psychological aspects of a new mosque in the neighborhood. By doing so, they ignore how the spatial and labor market relations are intertwined and how the reactions of sections of the neighborhood come from the idea the space is "theirs only." The problem is not as much in the disciplinary or methodological approach, but rather in its epistemological and ontological proposal. While it is true that these studies reveal fundamental aspects required to understand conflicts, it is also true that they fall short in their effort to understand the phenomenon both by excluding space as a fundamental factor and by delimiting the analysis to the ideological and discursive plane of structuring and social dynamics.

Conflicts arising around the construction or opening of mosques have a vital spatial component because they are new or transformed buildings changing the sense of place in a neighborhood, which in turn is embedded in a historical and geographical context. This means that any analysis of a conflict *over* or *in* space, such as the mosque conflicts, must include spatial logics in the analysis. Therefore, one of the fundamental purposes of this book is to draw attention to these socio-spatial dynamics inherent in conflict over mosques. They are frequently relegated to a second plan, if not directly ignored, which means that the geographical and spatial nature of the issue is not examined.

At the same time, following the proposed approach, it is pertinent to speak of a double space-time aspect that is continuously present. In other words, the ontological basis of this analysis is that, as Albert Einstein proposed in his own time, space and time are co-constitutive. One can see the temporal aspect of this phenomenon in the passing and simultaneity of time, and the spatial aspect in migratory flows through space and the transformation of space. As co-constitutive concepts, the two are related and one cannot be conceived without the other; that is, space (or any phenomenon that occurs in or on it) cannot be conceived efficiently without considering its temporal unfolding, and vice versa. That is why this intersection between time and space becomes a primordial nexus and thus a transversal concept and the driving force behind this book. Furthermore, following the ideas of Jaume Franquesa (2007), this double space-time aspect is beneficial for understanding local-global processes.

METHODOLOGICAL APPROACH

This book is part of a case study in the style of the Manchester School. Inspired by the extended case method, initially proposed by Max Gluckman in his *Analysis of a Social Situation in Modern Zululand* (1958) and *The Ethnographic Praxis of the Theory of Practice* (1961), this text is an anthropological study of the local-global processes of contemporary capitalism, exposed as they are through the space-time nexus through a concrete case: the conflict caused by the construction of a mosque in the coastal town of Premià de Mar.

Throughout the twentieth century, several authors have argued that economic relations should be understood in their most global context (Wolf

1990; Wallerstein 1974). Wolf and Wallerstein referred to the world division of labor, international and imperial economic relations, and migratory
movements, among other phenomena. There are various interpretations
put forward by other scholars.[9] Some authors speak of a system of global
dominance over the local, that is, macro towards micro, others showed that it
was more a question of dialectical relations—the line of thought which this
research follows. Now, in order to not confer more relevance to either of the
two (micro or macro, local or global), since they should rather be conceived
of as two poles of a continuum, here we will speak of a *local-global tension*.
Accordingly, we will speak of *local-global processes*[10] throughout the book
to refer to the processes that constitute this tension. Nevertheless, let us first
explain what these processes are.

Even though some authors such as Appadurai (1996), Hannerz (1998) and
Robertson (1992) insist that other, that is, non-economic, processes work at
a global level, such as cultural ones,[11] here we are talking about all the economic and political processes. Despite the actual relevance of the other processes, here we will focus on the economic-political elements. This is mainly
because the approach adopted had to correspond to the axes of the object of
study: migratory movements, urban transformations, and political mobilization around cultural differences.

Regarding the methodological perspective, I follow the approach of Max
Gluckman (1958)[12] and the Manchester School. The proposal constitutes
examining a concrete case, the analysis of which is extended to a more global
context, moving back and forth between the perspectives as one informs the
other. It is an advantageous methodological proposal to articulate the complexity of an object of study constituted of local-global processes (Burawoy
1998, 2000; Kapferer 2005; Mitchell 2008; Werbner 1984), and that is why it
has been the foundation of the structure of this investigation.

Following Kapferer (2005, 92), who argued that "the event or situation
begins the process of analytical revelation," here the local conflict serves
as the fulcrum, a textbook example of a social situation composed of
local-global processes. Thus, the present adaptation of the method can be
considered a long-term case study, since the description of the case is not
based on participant observation but on intensive work in archives and the
analysis of relevant documents; furthermore, because temporal development
will play an essential role in the research.

To place the reader and me, as a researcher, together at a common starting
point, I have begun with a brief description of the case. In this way, we also
place ourselves at a starting point for a more extensive investigation of the
context where, apart from fieldwork carried out during the four months of
December 2009–March 2010, which included interviews and observations

made in the town and the specific neighborhoods, also relies on data searched and extracted from municipal and private archives.

I decided to limit my focus to the Maresme neighborhood, where the conflict and most of the related events took place. When analyzing the production of space (Lefebvre 1991) of the town and the particular neighborhood, to carry it out satisfactorily and be faithful to the proposed method, I also had to consider the other interrelated scales such as the town and the region. Therefore, as will be clear, the analysis will focus on the region, the town and the neighborhood, without blinkering itself with narrow particulars. The same happens when we talk about migratory movements and policies: all have an anchor and effect that will vary depending on the starting point of the analysis, a particular experience or vision that, despite everything, is always linked to others within the local-global tension.

So, as described previously, the *elements of the object of study* (understood through the local-global tension described above) to be contemplated are:

- urban transformations
- the structure of the labor market and the flow of migration
- the construction and mobilization of "cultural differences" and the significant symbols linked to them.

These have been conveyed through two axes of analysis: 1) migratory movements and transformations of the town and 2) cultural conflicts, which, as will be seen, correspond to the two chapters of analysis: chapters 3 and 4.

FIELDWORK: METHODS AND TECHNIQUES

The fieldwork was carried out over four months, from December 2009–March 2010, although I had previously done a few surveys and would do a few more at irregular intervals until August. During this period of fieldwork, I used the following techniques: participant observation; archival work; qualitative in-depth interviews, semi-structured in the case of formal ones, with a guide made for each informant according to the information that was expected to be obtained; and formal and informal conversations. Here I will limit myself to making observations about the methods and their implications for the result to facilitate constructive criticism of the material and the analysis.

The method and theoretical-methodological vision adopted in this work raise serious doubts about what we call the field and, therefore, of the fieldwork itself. When are we in the field and when does fieldwork begin? The first day one comes into contact with an informant? The first day I stepped foot in Premià de Mar? In my view, this is a complex question that it largely depends on the scale we think about and whether "unconscious fieldwork" is included or not. For example, it could be argued that a large part of the research began when I arrived in Spain for the first time in 2005. Although the experiences I had since my first arrival (the constant back and forth between Denmark and Spain, my travels throughout the country, my stays in Salamanca, Castelló de la Plana, and finally Barcelona) have not been part of conscious fieldwork, nor of the unit of concrete analysis, they have undoubtedly had a significant influence on my perceptions, and hence the observations that I have made. Despite this, now it is complicated to reflect on the actual consequences of those experiences; even so, it has allowed me to adopt certain ease of communication and to acquire more specific knowledge about the local-global context in question. It thus constitutes a first immersion, essential for subsequent work.

Likewise, my position as a researcher has been favorable for the swing between objectivity (or objectification as Bourdieu wrote in 2003) and subjectivity, external and internal, which must be pursued in ethnography. On the one hand, in meeting with my informants, it has been more normal for them to explain the practices and events of the town to me due to my characteristic of "being a foreigner." On the other hand, it has been much more feasible to adopt certain objectivity due to the lack of an apparent inclination towards one or another position within society.[13]

In the same way, it can be argued that I had an extended introduction to the field, an investigation of the larger context (Castelló de la Plana 2005–2007) and the more immediate (Barcelona 2008–2010). In these periods, I was not engaged in fieldwork in the strict sense; the knowledge acquired during the period preceding the fieldwork proper has nonetheless been crucial to the success of the project, to the point that I consider that it forms part of the work. That said, from now on, when I talk about fieldwork, I will refer to the formal fieldwork carried out in Premià de Mar.

At the beginning of the fieldwork in Premià de Mar, I moved around the town, observing the plan of the town, its architecture and, to a lesser degree, the social life. I paid attention above all to the structure of the town and the different neighborhoods in terms of their buildings, squares, services, shops and bars. Therefore, I began with a more general observation, but slowly, from the moment I located the Maresme neighborhood and the site where the construction of the mosque had been planned, I focused my attention on the area in question (from Gran Via upwards) with especial interest in the social relations.

So, part of my initial strategy was to get in touch with the people of the immediate area, go into bars, sit in the squares, and walk through the streets, "reading" the space and the daily practices of the people, hoping to get in touch with the inhabitants. Slowly, an observation strategy very close to what some authors have called 'floating observation' (Pétonnet 1982) emerged. In fact, I had been largely inspired by Manuel Delgado's (1999) appreciations of an ethnography of space and the theoretical-methodological considerations of Nadja Monnet (2002). When observing spatial practices, both users and material space must always be considered. But after a while, I decided to change my strategy since it seemed to me that it had not worked well, perhaps because the conflict over the mosque was still too sensitive a subject. Consequently, and after Professor Ignasi Terrades made it easier for me to get in touch with him, I met with Pep,[14] the "self-taught local historian." The first time I visited him at his home, I discovered he held a private archive, with all sorts of documents and newspaper clippings: the Gómez-Fontanills Archive. So, I decided to spend an initial period at the archive investigating all kinds of material about the town and its history (mainly newspaper articles, publications of the neighborhood associations, books, research, photos, and maps). Pep then put me in touch with several residents who might be relevant. In this way, Pep would become my "gatekeeper" (a term used in anthropology to refer to the introducer in context).

After I had spent time doing the archival work, I was finally able to get started with interviews and informal conversations. Among those interviewed were a user of the mosque; the spokesperson of the Associació Islàmica At-Tauba (AIAT); four "autochthonous" residents[15] of the neighborhoods of Maresme, Casc Antic, and Barri Cotet; the then coordinator of Social Services; a former councilor for culture and another councilor for urban planning; four participants of the Plataforma Premià per la Convivència; the coordinator of a social program at the evangelical church; and a local sociologist.[16]

Apart from the documents that I accessed through the Gómez-Fontanills Archive, I relied on information and documents from the Registry of Urban Planning of Catalonia (RPUC) including urban plans, land use planning, regulations, modifications, etc., town council documents (first occupation license, maps, urban plans, action plans, etc.), documents from the Premià de Mar municipal library (books, studies, action plans, AAVV magazines, etc.). I also had access to the minutes of the meetings of the Premià de Mar Neighborhood Associations Coordinator (CAV), and documentary materials such as *30 Minutes: A Mosque in Premià de Mar*, *¡Mesquita no!* and *La Mirada dels premianencs: passat, present i el futur de Premià de Mar*.

NOTES

1. As Moreras (2009, 46) says, we cannot be sure that there have not been previous conflicts. At the moment, we are only aware of the cases that have appeared in the media.

2. See Moreras (2009) and *¡Mezquita no!* (2005).

3. See Rincón (2008) and Cerote (www.webislam.com, 10/30/2008).

4. See Aixelà Cabré (2007).

5. Despite this, one of the hypotheses of Avi Astor, who says that the conflict has to do with the lack of community facilities and with a feeling of contempt, would not correspond to the case of Premià. In fact, the neighborhood was being restructured and improved precisely: the mosque had to be built together with the school, and the construction of both facilities would suppose, contrary to what some of the neighbors opposed to the construction said, an improvement of the environment, for example, on the road network.

6. Or this: "The neighbors ask that the mosque be installed 'on the outskirts' of the town to the concentration in a certain neighborhood 'of families with a religion and customs that contrast with the life and customs of those who are from here'" (Mancera 2001b).

7. Dídac is sixty-two years old, lives in the Casc Antic, Old Quarter, and took early retirement (previously he was a high school teacher). In addition, he was member of the Premià de Mar Neighborhood Associations Coordinator (CAV).

8. Take as an example the final report of the Community Development AEP (Pascual and Sánchez, 2005).

9. See Beck (1999) or Mintz (1998) for different and interesting treatments of this question.

10. This conceptualization underlines the dialectic between local and global and not, for example, the primacy of one over the other, and accentuates the procedural constituent of phenomena. This position also includes some of the criticisms made by Tsing (2000).

11. Appadurai (1996) for example mentions five "cultural (global) flows," while Hannerz (1998) speaks of three.

12. The most famous example is his study of the inauguration of a bridge in the north of what was once called Zululand. This shows the context of the particular society from which considerations about social structure, relationships and institutions can be extracted (Gluckman 1958).

13. Just to be clear, I do not believe that there is an absolute objectivity. Objectivity is an ideal that must be pursued in science. I also do not believe that a researcher can enter a field without positioning himself in one way or another.

14. Pep was then sixty-seven years old and lived in the garden area of the Eixample neighborhood. He was retired and had previously worked as an electrician, in a factory, and at the Stamping Museum. Furthermore, he was, among other things, a

self-taught artist and historian. The names that appear throughout the book have been anonymized.

15. Non-empirical category that arose in the 1990s in contrast to that of immigrants or foreigners and that does not make a distinction between Spanish and Catalan or class.

16. I never managed to meet with the representatives of the AAVV of Maresme and Bañeras, since they never answered my phone calls or the emails I sent. Also, it was relatively late when, for the first time, I was able to speak to someone from the mosque. These and other complications that I experienced were surely the result of the bad experiences they had had with the media over the years.

Chapter 1

Conflicts over the Construction of a Mosque in Premià de Mar

In 1987, Ramadan was celebrated for the first time, officially and publicly, in Premià de Mar, a small town located on the coast of the Maresme region, 30 kilometers north of Barcelona.[1] Premià de Mar is the setting for this story and the research that is in the background of this book. In the year of the first public Ramadan, a Muslim resident of Premià decided to buy a basement in Verge de Núria Street in the Maresme neighborhood,[2] and at the same time an association, Islamic Association At-Tauba (AIAT), was founded for the management of the premises that would function from then on as a mosque and a madrasa, a Koranic and Arabic school.[3]

At its foundation in 1987, AIAT requested permission to operate as an oratory in the basement of Verge de Núria Street, permission that was granted by the local council led by the mayor Josep Torrents i Morales[4] in 1988. It was not until about five years later when they received the first complaints from the neighbors about the operation of the oratory. Although these complaints date back to 1993, it took two years until some residents of the block[5] decided to address the town council, and thus, in 1995 the new council, led by the Partit Socialista de Catalunya (PSC)[6] under Maria Jesús Fanego Lorigados, managed to have an inspection of the premises carried out. As a consequence, in November 1996, the decision of the previous government was reversed and the cessation of religious activities was ordered owing to the lack of a municipal license and an alleged lack of security. The order, despite this, was not made effective due to allegations of those affected, the AIAT, who filed an administrative dispute that was accepted. At the same time, in December 1996, the community of owners convened a meeting of neighbors in the same room where the plenary sessions of the town council were held. One of the items on the agenda read "before further investment is made in the property, the community must approve whether or not to grant permission for foreign neighbors to remain under the leasing regime" (Juanola 1997).[7] In spite of everything, in the same article the board made assurances that they

> are not racist, it is a misunderstanding. The Catalan neighbors of the block maintain that foreigners smell bad and that they are very dirty . . . The harshest criticisms, however, focus on a mosque located on the ground floor. The Catalan residents assure that it does not have a permit and that the Mayor has issued an order for its closure.

Next, the town council and SOS Racismo met with the neighbors. Even so, some of the neighbors decided to go to court where they complained about the noise produced in the premises, a case that they nevertheless ended up losing (Gabinet d'Estudis Socials [GES] 2002, 10). In February 1997, because of the complaints and AIAT allegedly not complying with regulations, the town council ordered the closure of the oratory (Oró Badia 2004, 2).

Faced with the unsustainable situation in the block created by the tension with the neighbors and the growing demand for space, the AIAT decided to search for an alternative location; a task frustrated by the refusal of different owners to rent them a space. Because of these difficulties or rather the existing racism in the housing field—a phenomenon that racialized people have experienced for decades although it has only recently been "discovered" in the social and academic spheres[8]—the AIAT changed its strategy and began to look for land where they could build a new mosque. At the same time, the redevelopment and renovation of the Verge de Núria premises began, and despite its defects and limited space it would be a temporary premises for the duration of the search for another location and the works required to transform the new property into a place of worship. After a few months, the AIAT found a plot of land at 121–123 Joan Prim Street, just 250 meters from their original premises. It was a parcel of land classified for community buildings, and the first action as interested parties, alongside Pilar Docent S.L., who wanted to build a convent school, would be to ask the town council for a report on the use of the site.

The report was issued on May 2, 1997, with a positive response towards the construction of a mosque and a school next door.[9] Thus, the Premià de Mar mosque was to be the first newly built mosque in Catalonia. The foundation purchased the land and immediately afterwards the town council ordered the drafting of a special plan.

According to this plan, Pla Especial de deplegament d'una zona d'equipaments (The Special Plan for the Development of Community Buildings 1997),[10] the site in question is made up of half a block, delimited by Joan Prim Street, Mercè Street, Cisa Street, and the Passage Prim, which forms part of the Eixample area (see Figure 1.2). The other half of the block

Figure 1.1: The lot on Joan Prim.
Source: Martin Lundsteen (2010).

Figure 1.2: Surroundings of the mosque.
Source: Google Maps (2016).

is occupied by buildings two to four stories high, mainly private homes. The portion in question faces an area of semi-detached houses and was undeveloped.

At the time of the report's writing (1997), two urban planning actions were being carried out in the immediate surroundings:

The transformation of an industrial area into a residential area on the premises of the current cold-storage buildings known as Can Masriera, located on the opposite side of Joan Prim Street two blocks lower, and the refurbishment of the urban area known as Tarter-Fornells that will extend La Sisa and Montserrat Streets, among others, and will add important green areas between both streets. (The Special Plan for the Development of Community Buildings 1997)

THE SPECIAL PLAN

According to the plan, the interested parties were to bear the costs of the sidewalk improvements, street furniture, and street lighting. The budget for the improvement works was 3,126,130 pesetas (equivalent in 2021 to €18,788.42) for building A, and 946,050 pesetas (€5,685.88) for building B. According to the plan, the intention was for the construction of the two buildings to be carried out in a single stage. The area of building B was to be 699m², with a ground floor, two upper floors, and a minaret. The report states that the impact on the area "will imply making the options for the use of the new equipment possible, in a diversification of alternatives" and continues: "The equipment will affect the population in the aspect of enabling an alternative, which in no case can mean a pejorative condition. The use proposed by the equipment usually provides positive connotations to the immediate environment by improving the standard of services available to the residential areas."

The plan endorsed by the College of Architects of Catalonia (CAC) on June 25, 1997, was provisionally approved by the plenary session of the town council on October 15, 1997, and definitively approved by the Barcelona Urban Planning Commission (CUB) on November 5 before being published on December 17, 1997.

In addition, by trawling through the town council documents, I have been able to confirm that several building permits were issued at the same time for the city garden area nearby, where, as detailed in the Special Plan: "Recently a small urban intervention has taken place in the front of the area covered by this Special Plan, consisting of the extension of Carrer de la Sisa, from Carrer Joan Prim to Carrer Elisenda de Moncada. Likewise, the site is classified for General Community Facilities (key 5), so the permitted uses are: a) teaching, b) religious, and c) sociocultural."

In the archive we find time and again mention of Pilar Docent S.L. and the Islamic Cultural Center "Alttauba Mosque." These are the agents who proposed dividing the site into two parts: one, the largest, for the construction of the educational center (parcel A), and another, smaller, for the construction of the mosque (parcel B). The mosque proposed in the Special Plan is lower than usually allowed, but in addition to the construction of the two buildings, the expansion of Joan Prim Street is planned to create "a 'pedestrian' strip capable of supporting the crowding of pedestrians in the streets during hours of entry and exit of the facilities." It continues, "This way, in this section of street the passage between the enclosed blocks to the garden city is made smoother."

In 1997, when the CAC signed the Special Plan, a second neighborhood mobilization began, this time against the construction on Joan Prim Street. It was, however, the council's reaction to this mobilization that made the conflict experience its first *jumping scale*,[11] going from being a problem of the apartment block in question to being a neighborhood "problem." As we will see later, this rescaling was also a reaction of some residents to the neighborhood's changing demographics and socio-spatial reconfiguration. In any case, the local council then decided to propose a new location for the AIAT: next to the Santa María church[12], where there was indeed an undeveloped lot for the building of community facilities.[13] However, with this proposal, the council began a dangerous game of "hot potato" with the mosque's location.

Be that as it may, the new proposal renewed opposition to the building of the mosque and the residents of the new area submitted 1,500 signatures in objection, although due to the proximity of the church of Santa María, which is only a few streets away from Joan Prim and Verge de Núria, it is very likely that they were the same individuals as before and had already taken against the previous location. In fact, throughout the conflict, there was a cloud of uncertainty around the origin of many of the signatures collected; there were suspicions that signatures on the petition against the construction in Joan Prim Street were being recycled, or that, as reported by María Jesús Cañizares (2002), in the case of a grandfather who had signed but was not against the construction, the canvassers had concealed the real purpose of the petitions.[14]

During this first phase of the conflict, the residents who took a stance against the development were an anonymous group, which would not have been possible had they been an entity, association, or political party. They were without any clear motivation, even though it seems that the arguments that had the most weight were based on economics, an attitude that was "encouraged by a construction company with real estate interests in the area, which argued that the construction of the mosque would lower the value of the flats" (GES 2002, 11). Given the lack of specificity, we will allow the diffuse "oppositional neighbors" to remain, with the understanding that they were residents of Premià de Mar in general and not necessarily those who lived near to where the mosque was to be built, and that they did not, as yet, have any "organic existence" as such.[15]

After objections were raised to putting the mosque next to the church of Santa María, the town council decided to propose a new location. Instead of going back to the beginning, it proposed that it be built in a new industrial zone that was in the planning phase. However, the AIAT opposed the change and claimed its right to be able to build on the original site in Joan Prim. After some wrangling, the town council and the AIAT reached a provisional agreement. The AIAT still lacked sufficient funds to build the mosque[16] and had started a fundraising campaign. In the meantime, they would be able to continue using the premises on Verge de Núria Street with a separate entrance. For their part, the owners of the Joan Prim lot received threats from some neighbors (Cañizares 2002).

Later, in January 2000, a resident called for a demonstration against what she termed "violent immigrant groups" in the Maresme neighborhood on the same street as the mosque. There emerged very different motivations, including social assistance: "why do they [immigrants] receive social assistance when we don't?" There was an even broader context, including the events of Ca n'Anglada, which had taken place half a year previously (July 1999), a few weeks before the deaths of two farmers in El Ejido, and a few weeks after the media outbreak surrounding that conflict.[17] The apparent reason why the resident decided to call for the demonstration was that her son had been attacked on January 15 by a person from the Maghreb (Carles 2000).

The same neighbor then decided to call the demonstration off, purportedly for fear of an escalation of violence during the demonstration, since even people from outside Spain had contacted her to share their plans on joining in to "brutishly kill people." At the same time, the government warned her of "the significant fine that she would have to pay if any incidents occurred" (Carles 2000). However, it was too late. Despite her calling off the demonstration, there were intense clashes between people who appeared to be neo-Nazis and others from the Young Antifascist Platform who had brought together some 200 people, many of them youths, some with their faces covered (Carles 2000). They carried a banner that read: *No aggression, no racism. Premià for Convivencia!* The government sent approximately 70 members of the Rural Agents of the Civil Guard, the journalist's narration continued, remarking that everything passed without incident until "a few dozen of young people with a skinhead look from other towns appeared." That was the first of the violent confrontations in which the police intervened—clashes that continued throughout the night and resulted in three minor injuries and considerable property damage.

At the end of 2000, the Superior Court of Justice of Catalonia agreed with the town council and informed the AIAT that they had to close the premises permanently (Arenós and de la Fuente 2001). The town council then offered itself as a mediator in the search for new premises that would be offered to them through a short-term assignment. In the meantime, the community could stay in the old premises in Verge de Núria. Months later, on April 1, 2001, the council proposed a premises of about 50 m² located in Barri Cotet. The assignment would last until December of the same year, at which time "the town council and the entity would have to reach a 'definitive solution'" (Tarramera 2001). The AIAT accepted the proposal, although in passing they stated that the place did not meet their needs; it was too small. In a meeting with some of the residents of the neighborhood, in which the town council proposed the temporary location, the residents expressed that "the massive arrival of immigrants [was] worrying" and that they were against the construction of a mosque "wherever it may be" (Tarramera 2001). Although the neighborhood association was in favor of helping believers—in fact, its president José Molina said that "the neighborhood association has to respect all cultures"—in the end they decided to claim the locale for neighborhood activities. This position was owing to, firstly, the divergences of opinion between the board and some neighbors, and, secondly, that they had been trying to get the premises for years for themselves. Finally, and in response to the demand and position of the AAVV of Barri Cotet, the town council gave them the premises claiming that they did so "due to fear of a neighborhood conflict," and said that the community might occasionally request the use of a public space as they usually did during Ramadan (de la Fuente 2001a).

Thus, in April 2001 the Muslim community still did not have an alternative location with ten days to go before they would be forced to leave the premises (the proposed eviction date was April 20). At that time the AIAT decided to write to the Moroccan embassy asking them for their help in solving the problem (de la Fuente 2001a). Meanwhile, the Association of Moroccan Immigrant Workers in Spain (ATIME) issued a statement in which it affirmed that "the matter of the mosque in Premià exemplifies the growing wave of 'Islamophobia' that, in their opinion, is increasingly present in Catalonia" (Palou 2001). It is therefore evident that we are seeing the second scale change in the conflict: i.e., from it being once a local issue, actors operating at other scales have now become involved to turn it into a conflict in Catalonia.

The information presented by the AIAT and the town council about the granting of building permits is contradictory. It was held that AIAT did not have enough money to meet the expenses of the construction of the mosque as it wanted. Then the AIAT called for a peaceful demonstration on April 20, the day the premises were to be closed. However, the day before the eviction, the council announced that it would not close the premises; to do so was outside of the scope of its powers. They forbade the community to pray in the mosque and "put the matter in the hands of the judges and the police" (Palou and Tarramera 2001). From that moment the possible sale of the premises would be a continuous threat. The community was placed in a situation where, after thirteen years of using it, the premises no longer met their needs and they were, at least in theory, banned from it. In addition, they had spent time looking for alternative premises, and the only thing they found was that no one wanted to rent them any space. Moreover, the community's preferred solution to a stressful and discriminatory situation, i.e., the construction of a new mosque on the site of Joan Prim Street, could not be carried out due to political reluctance and then to economic limitations. For this reason, in 2001, after almost fifteen years in the area, the Muslims, whether they were believers or not, Moroccans, Senegalese, Gambians, or converts,[18] from Premià de Mar or nearby,[19] found themselves without their own premises in which to meet and pray.

On the same day, April 20, the AIAT decided to stage a sit-in at the premises until the town council gave them an alternative location where they could pray. The council's answer came a few hours later: settle in some prefabricated modules. Although its location had yet to be specified, it would be on the outskirts of the city. Meanwhile, the construction of the mosque would begin, adjusted to the congregation's budget, an agreement in which the Consell Islàmic Cultural de Catalunya intervened. The initial deadline to confirm the location of the prefabricated modules was one week, but the parties immediately saw that the time limit was impossible given the many procedural matters to be completed. For the time being, they would continue to use the premises on Verge de Núria Street.

Let us pause to introduce a new actor in the drama: the Consell Islàmic Cultural de Catalunya (Islamic Cultural Council of Catalonia or CICC) was created in 2001. At the time, it was the only federation of Muslim communities established in Catalonia,[20] and was founded with the purpose of acting as an interlocutor with Catalan institutions (Prado 2008, 177–182, 256–257). At that time, it was very well regarded by the Generalitat, since it had long wanted to establish relations between the Muslim religious communities in Catalonia. In fact, in the absence of alternatives, it seemed to them that the CICC offered a minimum of representation and consequently signed a collaboration agreement with it, by which, among other things, it "established that the CICC [would] collaborate with the Generalitat in matters related to the rights of religious freedom and that affect the Muslim community of Catalonia. In exchange, the Generalitat [would] participate with an economic contribution for the maintenance of the entity." (Prado 2008, 178). Therefore,

CICC's arrival on the scene was coupled with the Generalitat's own interest in intervening in the conflict, and with the desire of the Premià de Mar Town Council that the Generalitat do so.

We return to the story. After a month, they had still not found land on which to place the temporary prefabricated modules—in fact, they never would. Meanwhile, the residents who opposed the mosque continued to collect signatures against the construction of the Joan Prim site by canvassing the town's shops (bars, butchers, etc.) and knocking on doors; a mobilization that was beginning to bear fruit, since they claimed they already had 5,500 signatures against construction (Mancera 2001a). The town council, for its part, expressed the intention of bringing together all the neighborhood associations in a commission to seek a consensus, another project that was never formalized. For its part, the AIAT presented a new works plan, for which it requested the necessary permits (construction and activity licenses).

The original plan for the mosque had set out a building of three stories, plus a basement. The new plan was, however, adjusted for the AIAT's budgets, which meant that it would comprise a basement, a ground floor, and a loft (Figure 1.3). In total, it would be about "230 m² of habitable space with a capacity of 115 prayer places for men and 33 for women" (Juanola 2001) with an estimated price of €193,000.

In response to the entry of the project in the municipal registry, the opposing residents summoned the presidents of the Premià de Mar neighborhood associations. Only three attended: the Banyeres neighborhood, Barri Cotet and the Farrerons neighborhood. The president of the Farrerons only stayed for a few minutes, as what she heard displeased her so much that she decided to leave before the meeting even started (Juanola 2001).

The council's decision regarding the licenses would not be made until September 2001, even though the then town planning councilor said that "he [would] authorize the permit if the project [complied] with the regulations, but [would] not rule out proposing a land swap" (Mancera 2001a). Or, as reported in an article in *La Vanguardia* of the same day: "We are willing to find a solution to avoid confrontations" (de la Fuente 2001b). A few months later, in September 2001, the famous attacks on the Twin Towers in New York took place, events that did nothing more than cultivate a hostile environment towards the Muslim population in general, and everything that could be associated with Islam, thus promoting Islamophobic discourses (Cesari 2006).

In October 2001, after almost a year of searching for a new location and eight months after agreeing to move temporarily to the prefabricated modules on the outskirts of town, a judge ordered the closure of the premises and left the Muslims of Premià without a home. They had found no viable solution and they continued to pray at the premises on Verge de Núria Street. Initially, AIAT decided to comply with the court order, but asked the town council

El projecte del nou temple musulmà preveu que podrà acollir a la vegada entre 200 i 300 fidels

Estel Batet
PREMIÀ DE MAR

El disseny de la mesquita de Premià es negociarà amb els veïns

La comunitat islàmica vol pactar el color o si hi fa un minaret

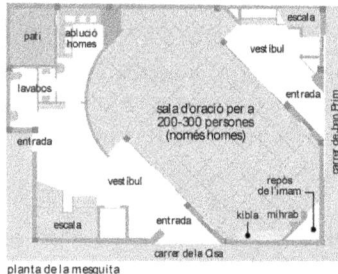

La comunitat islàmica Alttauba ja disposa dels plànols del projecte de construcció de la mesquita al carrer .ban Prim, que ara es negocia si serà l'emplaçament definitiu per al temple. Ja hi ha llicència, projecte i se n'estudia el pressupost, però de moment les obres quedaran congelades mentre no acabi el procés de negociacions entre els musulmans, l'Ajuntament i els veïns.

El solar del carrer .ban Prim té 227 metres quadrats i el centre de culte ocuparà una superfície de 220 m², repartits en una planta baixa de 216 m² i un soterrani que servirà com a magatzem de 220 m². El temple també tindrà un altell, que és on resaran les dones, que només hi aniran els divendres i els caps de setmana per escoltar el discurs de l'imam. "És preferible que les dones resin a casa; és el marit el que els dóna els consells a seguir", explica Rachid Woudah, membre del col·lectiu islàmic.

En principi, el projecte estava plantejat per tenir planta baixa

planta de la mesquita

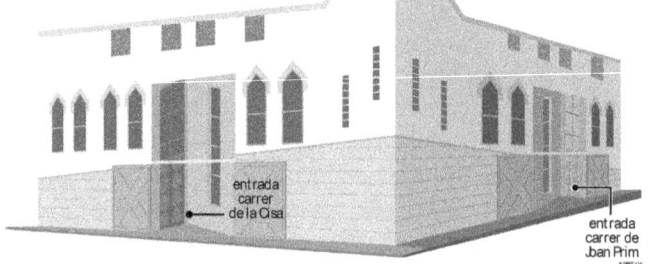

EL TEMPLE DEL CARRER JOAN PRIM

El projecte de la mesquita preveu construir una planta baixa i un altell. En una segona fase s'ampliaria construint-hi més pisos.

La comunitat musulmana té previst obrir el temple al públic un cop cada quinze dies

i dos pisos, però la manca de pressupost va obligar els musulmans a reduir l'obra.

El projecte de la mesquita no inclou en principi cap minaret. "Negociarem amb els veïns si posar minaret o no i també el color de la façana", van explicar els musulmans. Es tracta d'una obra modesta, amb una façana semblant a la d'una església i que només denota la seva utilitat per l'estètic de les finestres, que són una simplificació dels arcs típics de l'arquitectura àrab: arrodonits i acabats en punxa. La façana del carrer .ban Prim tindrà quatre finestres i la del tram del carrer de la Cisa, que encara s'ha d'obrir, en tindrà sis.

L'espai principal de la mesquita l'ocuparà la sala d'oració dels homes, que ocuparà un total de 105,80 metres quadrats.

Destaca també la sala d'ablució dels homes, que tindrà 15 metres quadrats. Aquest espai és el que els musulmans utilitzen per rentar-se abans de resar. Tal com mana l'Alcorà, abans de fer les oracions els seguidors de l'Islam s'han de rentar per purificar-se.

El projecte també inclou dos vestíbuls, un pati de vuit metres quadrats, una sala més d'oració i un espai perquè l'imam hi reposi.

L'alçada màxima que pot tenir l'edifici és d'11,55 metres quadrats, tal com manen les normatives per als espais d'equipaments.

Si el projecte s'amplia, les plantes superiors del temple podrien acollir una llibreria i un espai per fer classes de llen-

gua i cultura àrabs a tothom que hi estigui interessat, però sobretot aniran adreçades als fills dels immigrants. Els musulmans tenen la intenció d'obrir el temple al públic un cop cada quinze dies perquè la gent conegui de prop la mesquita i pugui consultar alguns llibres.

La capacitat d'aforament serà d'entre 200 i 300 persones. Tot i això, Rachid Woudah destaca que normalment són pocs els que van a resar.

Els divendres, quan es fa el prec més important de la setmana, com a molt es congreguen un centenar de musulmans. Per dates assenyalades com és el Ramadà o el Dia del Xai la comunitat islàmica demanarà a l'Ajuntament que els cedeixi un espai més gran on hi tingui cabuda la gran quantitat de gent que es reuneix per a aquestes celebracions.

Els musulmans desmenteixen que la mesquita, tot i que sigui la primera oficial que es construeix a Catalunya, atregui una allau de musulmans d'arreu. "Cadascú té la seva mesquita i la majoria de nosaltres no tenim temps de desplaçar-nos des del lloc on treballem cada vegada que hem de resar", explica Redouan Toujgani.

Els musulmans resen cinc vegades al dia: una a les 6 del matí, que és la menys seguida, a les 2 del migdia, a les 6 de la tarda, a un quart de 10 del vespre, la més multitudinària, i la darrera a un quart d'11 de la nit. Tot i això, Radouan comenta que "el 90 per cent dels musulmans resen a casa seva per comoditat".

Els arquitectes: "Un encàrrec poc habitual"

L'any 1997, l'equip d'arquitectes format per JD. i F.T. va rebre l'encàrrec per part de la comunitat islàmica Alttauba de fer el projecte de la mesquita, la primera oficial de Catalunya. "Al principi ens va sorprendre perquè no és un encàrrec habitual", explica un dels arquitectes. "Era una proposta molt temptadora amb certa repercussió", tot i que reconeix que no s'esperaven que fos tan polèmica. JD. assegura que com a arquitectes van valorar més el repte que significava construir un temple

religiós que no les conseqüències que podia comportar. Elaborar el projecte no va ser una tasca gens fàcil. Un dels primers passos a seguir per elaborar un projecte arquitectònic és inspirar-se en construccions semblants, i en aquest cas es van haver de desplaçar fins a València per conèixer com és un temple musulmà, quines pràctiques s'hi duen a terme i quins són els hàbits religiosos de l'Islam.

Paral·lelament, JD. i F.T. van recopilar una gran quantitat de documenta-

ció sobre l'Islam i les mesquites. Després de moltes reunions amb la comunitat musulmana, fa un any i mig el projecte es va acabar i ja fa mesos que es va presentar a l'Ajuntament de Premià de Mar. "Va ser un procés lent que havia de madurar, però els musulmans tampoc tenien pressa", comenta l'arquitecte. La característica principal del projecte és que l'interior de l'edifici està dissenyat perquè tot estigui orientat cap a la Meca.

Avui, 2002-06-03, p. 22.
Servei de Gestió Documental, Arxius i Publicacions de l'Ajuntament de Girona (www.girona.cat/sgdap)

Figure 1.3: Drawings of the mosque.
Source: Avui, Hermes Comunicacions S.A. (Batet 2002).

for an alternative place to celebrate Ramadan, which was about to begin. In response, representatives of the town council met with those of the AIAT, the CICC and the Secretari d'Afers Religionales (SAR) of the Generalitat de Catalunya and an agreement was made. In exchange for ceasing activities at the premises on the ground floor,[21] the town council would give them the premises of the old Escola Voramar (see location in Figure 1.4) for the month of Ramadan and two further sites (according to the town council, construction was planned). In addition, a monitoring commission would be created to deal with "issues related to the Muslim community, including the construction of a mosque" (de la Fuente 2001c). It was to be a commission that "would meet regularly to deal with cultural and social issues that [affected] the Muslim community both in terms of the population of Premià de Mar and the rest of Catalonia. This commission [would] be made up of the Generalitat, the Town Council of Premià de Mar, the Islamic Council, and those responsible for the mosque in Premià de Mar" (Ansola 2001).

A few weeks later, and on the same day that the mosque project was publicly presented, a group of residents delivered 5,554 signatures against the construction and requested that the council deny the permit for a mosque on Joan Prim Street. "Neighbors, who refuse to provide identities and want to remain anonymous [to the press], claim that the site, which is owned by the Muslim community, is inappropriate because of its location. They also

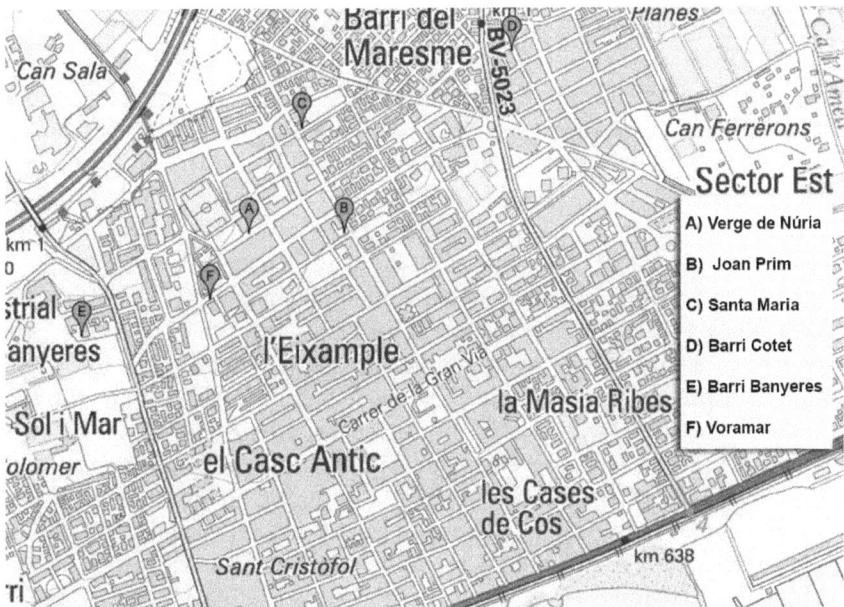

Figure 1.4: Map of the locations.
Source: Author's own elaboration from Catalan Institute of Cartography and Geoinformation (ICGC) (2010).

wonder why Muslims should be allowed to practice their religion 'in the center of town'" (Bernabé and Ribet 2001).

Despite an apparent homogeneity, it must be specified that this group of residents was divided into two factions, one that opposed only the construction on Joan Prim Street and the other that opposed construction anywhere. On the same dates, leaflets by the Plataforma "No a la Mesquita en la calle Joan Prim (Platform "No to the Mosque on Joan Prim Street" or PNM-JP) were distributed calling for a demonstration that would never be held. It is of note that in the pamphlets signed by the said platform 1) there was an image of a majestic mosque, 2) they argued that the council, secretly, had rezoned the land to make the construction of the mosque possible, and 3) they alerted the population of the arrival of thousands of Muslims to Premià de Mar.

Faced with this situation, the mayor decided to turn the screw again and advised that they talk again about a possible relocation of the mosque; with the intention to avoid further conflicts, AIAT was willing to negotiate the matter, so long as its interests were respected. On November 18, the territorial delegate of the Generalitat in the regions of Barcelona and Secretary of Religious Affairs, Ignasi Garcia Clavel, asked for more "flexibility" on the part of the Muslim community, and a few weeks later, the town council asked that AIAT request the suspension of the construction work permit for the mosque on Joan Prim and that the site be moved to another located in the future industrial estate in the Banyeres neighborhood. This would set a precedent in the following years.

In the beginning, the members of PNM-JP were satisfied with the proposal, while AIAT undertook to study it, albeit with suspicion, and highlighted that it had already accrued expenses that it would not recover (Batet 2001). Despite this, since the land in the Banyeres neighborhood was still industrial land it would have to be rezoned (a process that could take up to two years), AIAT insisted that the council offer them a place to go for the duration of the construction (Bernabé 2001). CICC spoke out against the proposal and maintained that the only solution was to build on the site that AIAT had purchased (Batet 2001). Meanwhile it was agreed that the usage of the Escola Voramar would be extended until February. In the end, AIAT decided not to accept the transfer, suspended negotiations and put the matter in the hands of its lawyer, because the town council said it did not have any provisional sites. Next, the town council requested an extension of the administrative procedure to grant the license thus the decision was postponed for four months. Meanwhile, the residents of the Banyeres neighborhood met with the town council.

At the beginning of 2002, the town council reached an agreement with the owners of the land in the Banyeres neighborhood to define a partial development plan for the area. Despite this, during the following month, some of the residents of the future polygon collected a petition of about 700 signatures against the mosque. Again "the neighbors" were a varied group and, according to the journalist Emma Ansola, they came from "Barrio Banyeres Street and [there were] the owners of the houses located on the Premià de Dalt Road, on Maresme Street and in Nou Premià," but there were also signatories from residents of the city center (Ansola 2002a).

Among the arguments of these opponents, greatest weight was given to the loss in value of real estate while they refused even to mention racism. In fact, some residents consulted by *El Mundo* (Cedó Garcia 2002a), "suspected that the construction of luxury single-family homes near the industrial estate may 'have [had] a lot to do with it' as they 'cost about €40 million each' and they believed that 'the mosque [would] lower the value of the property.'" A few weeks later, 800 more signatures were added to bring the total to 1,500 (Cedó Garcia 2002b). This time the town council announced that it would not back down, and that this location would be the final one, provided that AIAT agreed; in addition, the AIAT was told that they could remain at the Escola Voramar campus until June. The AIAT continued to negotiate through its lawyer.

We are about to enter the tensest months of the conflict, but before proceeding, it is worth summarizing what has happened so far. AIAT has been in negotiations with the town council since 2000 and has not yet found a viable and lasting solution for the location of the new mosque. At first, AIAT bought land in Joan Prim Street with the council's explicit guarantee that they would be allowed to build a mosque, since the land was classified as land for community buildings. Despite their promise, with time and facing neighborhood protests, the council's statements became increasingly ambiguous, and AIAT decided to break direct negotiations with the council, leaving them in the hands of its lawyer. Undoubtedly, the council did not help to reduce the tension between the parties, rather they indicated, albeit indirectly, that the Muslims were the party causing the conflict. If one thing is clear, it is that the ambivalence has served to unite the opposition, since more and more people were opposed to the future construction of a mosque.

The most critical period began when, in the middle of April 2002, the town council announced that it wanted to evict the Muslims from the Escola Voramar campus. AIAT had not accepted the proposal to move to the industrial park for two main reasons: firstly, they did not like having to give up the building permit for the lot on Joan Prim Street, and, secondly, because the council had not fulfilled its promise to offer the congregation a secure place of worship while planning and building the new mosque in the Banyeres neighborhood. The council decided that the negotiations had failed and on April 12, it notified AIAT that they had 48 hours to vacate the Escola Voramar campus. AIAT met with CICC and the Moroccan consulate,[22] but both were agreeable to the transfer (for unknown reasons, the CICC had changed its

position). AIAT interpreted these meetings and the CICC's shift as retalia-
tion, namely that they had only entered dialogue with them to apply pressure
on the opposition's behalf. The AIAT's lawyer, Silvia Iniesta, presented an
appeal in court, on the basis that the town council had abused its power. She
recommended to AIAT that they use their lot on Joan Prim Street for prayers.
The town council later warned the community leadership that they were not
permitted to pray at the site and a report from the municipal technical engineer
warned that doing so could mean they would be sanctioned (Ribet 2002b).

A few days after the Muslim congregation had vacated the Escola Voramar
campus, some residents of Banyeres blocked the road between Premià de
Mar and Premià de Dalt, in protest against the council's decision to allow the
mosque to be built in the area. AIAT spokesman Rachid Wouddah said that
he was now convinced that "the only solution [was] to build the mosque on
the Joan Prim Street site at once. 'Wherever we go, the situation will be the
same'" (Ribet 2002a). The plan now was to do the Friday prayers as an act of
protest at Joan Prim Street, and for this reason they cleaned the enclosure of
the litter and graffiti that had appeared over the previous days (Pérez 2002a).

Pamphlets signed by the PNM-JP began to appear calling for a "noisy
rally" against the construction of the mosque, timed to coincide with the
salat. On the same day, a press release appeared in *El Periódico* stating that:
"The mayor . . . announced yesterday that she [would] grant the license, by
'legal imposition' . . . to the community. Fanego [the mayor] expressed her
dissatisfaction with the council's general decision and said that the best thing
to do would be to build . . . in the Banyeres neighborhood" (Oñate 2002).
Later, a somewhat simplistic, and perhaps partisan, statement appeared in the
final document granting the license to build (Pérez Pons 2002):

> As representatives of the citizens of Premià de Mar, we have the obligation to
> ensure respect for religious freedom and worship in the municipality in accor-
> dance with the Spanish Constitution and the Law of Religious Freedom, and
> respect for urban regulations in force, therefore, we find ourselves with the obli-
> gation to grant the environmental license for the location of a Muslim Worship
> Center, by legal imperative.

Thus, the process closed, and the allegations presented by some neighbors
and the Platform "No to the Mosque on Joan Prim Street" were dismissed.[23]
However, about fifty believers came to the site at noon to pray, accompanied
by neighbors who carried banners saying, "NO to the mosque" or similar, and
one neighbor in particular with very loud music "trying to prevent the prayer
from being heard" (de la Fuente 2002). Some threw garbage into the lot
while others yelled and insulted the Muslims present. The prayer announced
for the afternoon was never carried out, probably due to the strong presence

of protesters who had gathered half an hour beforehand and the environment experienced previously. Because of the xenophobic attitudes of the neighbors and the implicit support of the town council of these behaviors, AIAT's lawyer, now Máximo Godó, said that he would denounce the town council and the people (Berlanga 2002). At the same time, he expressed "his discomfort at the way the protests unfolded, in which around three hundred residents of the town took to the streets, shouting slogans such as 'No to the mosque,' 'Go back home' and, 'May the Catholic Monarchs return,' they showed their rejection of the building of the mosque in the aforementioned premises at the center of town" (Berlanga 2002).

Owing to these actions and the strong media coverage they drew, the other inhabitants of Premià de Mar who had previously mobilized against fascism reorganized themselves. The anti-fascists had never ceased to exist, they were simply less organized. They met at La Amistad Center to organize a rally against racism and in favor of coexistence, and on Saint George's Day (*Diada de Sant Jordi* in Catalan, a very important holiday in Catalonia) some 50 people demonstrated in the Plaza del Ayuntamiento and read the "Manifesto for the Respect of Civil Rights" signed by the Coordinadora Premià per la Convivència (Coordinating Committee Premià in favor of Convivència or CPpC).[24] This interest group, a key actor in future events, comprised inhabitants and entities of Premià de Mar who expressed their concern about the continual erosion of social harmony and peace in the town and rejected the xenophobic attitudes of the neighbors opposed to the construction of the mosque, in addition to criticizing the actions of the town council. They also defended what they saw as the legitimate right of citizens to freedom of belief and worship, and demanded that the council promote and respect the rights and responsibilities of all citizens. They read the manifesto in the Plaza del Ayuntamiento and invited locals who shared this position to come to the Civic Center on April 26.

On the same day PNM-JP, the platform against the construction of the mosque on Joan Prim Street, also called for a rally, but they cancelled it because of "fear of the presence of radical groups." They also regretted "that they [were] branded as racists, because the only thing they criticized [was] the mosque's location" (Ansola 2002b), ran an explanation given by Bernat Gutiérrez, one of the neighbors opposed to the construction, and continued that there was, "some concern in the neighborhood because at eleven o'clock at night they are on the site praying in subhuman conditions" (Ansola 2002b).[25] Another neighbor acknowledged that, according to him, they were not interested in kicking the Muslims out, because there had never been a problem with them, rather the problem was with the construction of an "emblematic building," that could "lead to many people coming from outside" (Ansola 2002b). Despite the diversity in the opposition's opinion, it grew stronger and increasingly consistent as time went on.

The demonstration was announced once again, over the course of which the Plataforma per Catalunya (Platform for Catalonia or PxC) was present distributing pamphlets with overtly racist messages (Pérez 2002b). Likewise, Josep Anglada y Ríos, the leader of the Platform, was celebrated by some of the local residents opposed to the mosque, when he assured them that they were no longer "alone" and promising to call a large demonstration against the building in fifteen days' time (Cedó Garcia 2002c).

PLATFORM FOR CATALONIA (PXC)

Plataforma per Catalunya (PxC) is an organization whose values are a hybrid of the modern far right and traditional fascism. It was formally founded in January 2001 in Vic, with Josep Anglada y Ríos as its leader. In his own words, it is a "populist-identity party created specially to seek 'better control of immigration and more citizen security.'" Coinciding with the conflict, Josep Anglada was recorded with a hidden camera by Channel 9 (Autonomous Television of the Valencian Community). In the recording, Anglada explains his fascist ideology and his agreement with, for example, Marine Le Pen, Jörg Haider, and Pim Fortuyn, and acknowledges that he disguises himself as a democrat to win votes. One of his central ideas is what he dubs the "Islamist challenge." The "challenge" is a type of war of religions that began with the Crusades and the Reconquest and that, they claim, is still in force today. His appearance in conflicts such as that of Premià has been his primary political strategy ever since, and the discourse surrounding the conflict changes dramatically: although previously his "anti-Islamist" and "anti-Moor" discourse was only one of many positions the party took, now it is becoming the general posture of PxC.

Meanwhile, in April 2002, the spokespersons of all the municipal groups and political parties held a meeting to agree on a joint statement on the issue of the mosque. They presented a short statement in favor of tolerance and coexistence, as well as respect for fundamental rights: "Declaration for Convivencia in Premià de Mar" (PSC, CiU, PP, ERC, and IC-V de Premià de Mar 2002).

The town council's next move was to send a notice to the AIAT that demanded the congregation immediately cease using the site as a place of worship, to which the AIAT responded they would pray in the street. When the CPpC gathered at the Civic Center with more than 100 citizens of various backgrounds and representatives from at least twelve interest groups, they decided to call a gathering on May 2 followed by an organized demonstration on May 12. At the same time, Josep Anglada and PxC called for a demonstration against the mosque on May 18. For her part, the mayor reiterated that the town council would give permission for the works, but she added that she felt deceived by the Islamic community for not having accepted any of the alternatives.

At the rally on May 2, the CPpC brought together about 300 people and the manifesto was read in several languages on Sant Jordi. The CPpC also planned to create a forum for debate among all the parties involved. On May 7, 2002, the town council approved the building permit for the construction of the mosque.[26] The CPpC asked the rector of the parish of San Cristóbal to provide a place for the Muslim community for as long as they remained without a mosque. The rector responded that he would transfer the petition to the parish council, but later he informed them that it was not possible.

On the 12th, the demonstration called by the CPpC marched through the streets of Premià. About 1,000 people gathered and thirty local and state organizations joined in, including unions and NGOs. The Iniciativa per Catalunya-Verds (Initiative for Catalonia Greens or ICV)[27] was also out in force. According to the media, the demonstration had a festive feeling and there were no incidents, and they gave the event mostly positive reports.

Later, CICC returned to offer its opinion, saying that the Banyeres neighborhood was the best option and as a consequence AIAT disavowed its intervention. In the town council there were also problems. Apparently the leftist pact of the government was in danger because of ICV's position on the mosque. PSC and ERC did not accept the criticism that the CPpC had made of the council's actions, while ICV communicated that the pact had not been working well for some time and that the governing parties only wanted to take advantage of the controversy to justify the break. The pact survived, but the Territorial Services area was restructured, an area that ICV controlled. The city government finally authorized the demonstration to be held by Josep Anglada's party with neighbors opposed to the mosque. Incidentally, the party, PxC, already had a local branch called Plataforma per Premià de Mar (Platform for Premià de Mar or PxP). Antifascist Action circulated a call for a counter-demonstration, from which CPpC distanced itself.

On May 18, the demonstration finally took place, drawing between 1,000 and 1,500 people according to police sources. It was led by Anglada, whose presence the crowd cheered on Plaça dels Països Catalans. At the beginning of the demonstration there were incidents between protesters. Some had the shaved head and appearance of neo-Nazis and others were from Antifascist Action. The media did not hesitate to define it as a "battle royale" (Editorial Office, *ABC* 2002). Significantly, the police did not intervene. The following day, the town council called a meeting of all the political forces of the government and the opposition to confront what they define as a "social fracture" and find a consensus solution while making an appeal to the central government delegation and the Generalitat to intervene. As a consequence, a commission was formed to negotiate with the Muslim community. The Popular Party did not participate and blamed the town council for mismanaging the situation.

All Catalan political leaders made statements about the situation in Premià de Mar. Non-governmental organizations such as ATIME (Association of Moroccan Immigrant Workers in Spain) and SOS Racism warned of the presence of the extreme right in the conflict. The then secretary of ERC and member of the Catalan Parliament Josep-Lluís Carod-Rovira even called for the expulsion of the Imam of Premià de Mar, for being "anti-Catalan." In fact, a dispute began between Artur Mas, the then First Minister of Catalonia and Carod-Rovira, about which was the first to propose the expulsion of "radical imams" (Editorial Office, *La Vanguardia* 2002). The imam had, in fact, quit the country some years before. Despite the heat the comments appeared to give to the conflict, they did nothing other than show how out of proportion it had become. The question the community faced was no longer one of the location of a new mosque but of cultural and national identity.

The Generalitat de Catalunya publicly asked the Muslim community to postpone the start of the works and to return to the negotiating table to find a location that generated less opposition. The town council, for its part, once again offered them the Escola Voramar, from which they had already been expelled, as a preliminary step to the negotiations. AIAT's lawyer asked that the offer be made in writing by means of a decree by the mayor's office before May 31. The Muslims agreed to negotiate again, but made it clear that they did not want to build in the Banyeres neighborhood. The representative of PxC to Premià, Lluis Sadurní, made clear that they did not want the mosque anywhere at all. A few days after Anglada revealed on the Channel 9 program that he thought that democracy was the only legitimate path to power, the neighbors opposed to the mosque disassociated themselves from their party, despite the fact that they maintained the name of Plataforma per Premià. Later the party would change the name to Veïns Independents de Premià (Independent Neighbors of Premià or VIP).

The internal divisions of the residents against the mosque were once again being made visible. On the one hand, there were those who followed Anglada's line, with a discourse focused on the incompatibilities between cultures and the difficulties of *convivencia*, approaching it as a problem of migration and religion, and opposed to building the mosque anywhere. On the other hand, there were people who were against the construction on Joan Prim Street. These used more politically correct and technical arguments, emphasizing, for example, the supposed unviability on that street; according to them it did not fit the urban environment. They also worried about the central location of the mosque and the alleged problems of parking and human crowding that this new construction would bring, as well as fears of a drop in prices for homes in the area.

In June 2002, AIAT was still waiting for a written commitment from the town council, an agreement that was to include the commitments made by both parties. The Escola Voramar site was to be provisionally transferred to them for a period of five to fifteen years and AIAT had to cease plans to build on Joan Prim Street. But AIAT did not accept it, because they did not feel assured that the building permit could be renewed after its two-year validity. Meanwhile, the Associació de Veïns i Establiments del Casc Antic de Premià de Mar (Association of Neighbors and Establishments of the Old Town of Premià de Mar or AVECA) asked the town council to hold a referendum on the construction of the mosque.

After a few more months, it finally seemed that the parties had reached an agreement: AIAT agreed not to build the mosque on Joan Prim Street and in exchange the town council gave them the use of the Escola Voramar premises on a rental basis for fifteen years. The town council undertook to develop these premises and to rent the land on Joan Prim Street. It was agreed to make a mutual assignment, with neither party paying rent to the other, and in the meantime the building permit would be suspended. There was also talk of placing a Municipal Council for Coexistence on the campus of the Escola Voramar. The Generalitat expressed its support for this agreement. The PxP disliked the arrangement and called for another demonstration, but cancelled it at the last minute. The town council published an information brochure on the agreement which, announcing additionally a forthcoming Pacte per la Nova Ciudadania (Pact for a New Citizenship).

Yet in July 2002, the contract was still not signed. There were details to negotiate, such as, for example, what would happen to the AIAT if no agreement had been reached on the location of the mosque at the expiry of their lease of the school. CPpC expressed its dissatisfaction with the agreement at a press conference, in addition to complaining that they had been excluded from the negotiations. They believed that the Escola Voramar site did not offer a viable solution and that the mosque had to be built on Joan Prim Street, despite the fact that it also ensured that it would respect the agreement if the congregation accepted it.

On September 5, 2002, the agreement between the town council and AIAT was signed. Among the signatories were the mayor, the secretary of the Muslim community, the secretaries of Religious Affairs of the Generalitat de Catalunya, and the CICC. The opposition parties did not attend, nor did the other partners of the government (ERC and ICV). As a condition of the agreement, the Pact for a New Citizenship was signed. The pact served as a "commitment of its signatories to work for a city model based on social cohesion, *convivencia*, citizenship and equal opportunities, and that responds to the new needs and changes that immigration represents."

Even so, a few days later, Premià de Mar, El Masnou, Mataró and Pineda de Mar signed a collaboration agreement with the Generalitat de Catalunya for the implementation of a Regional Immigration Plan. In that month's Plenary of the Town Council, the pact was approved and a declaration of principles of the political parties on the subject of immigration was composed. The Consell Municipal per la Convivència (Municipal Council for Coexistence) was constituted as a body that would work on proposals and projects related to immigration. It was made up of municipal groups and entities and associations that wanted to participate. The AIAT was thus put at a disadvantage by their decision to forego their right and settle in a municipal premises to allow the conflict to be temporarily settled. The local government put into place an infrastructure, the council, and discursive devices around the subject of "the immigrant" which would target and somehow blame the "cultural other." I will return to this topic in chapter four.

Through this historical overview of the conflict we have been able to see how a small-scale conflict with very particular characteristics changed in scale and character. Slowly, and due to the interventions by the different agents involved, be that the administrations, local or regional associations or social movements, the framing of the question and the speeches transformed a neighborhood conflict of one little block into one depicted as a conflict concerning migration and cultural diversity; a narrative in which everyone more or less participated, from all over the political spectrum. Now, despite the insistence of some actors in presenting Muslims as problematic, there were also those who defended the fundamental rights of the new residents. In a similar way, although contrary to many simplistic accounts that represented the protesters as simple racists, some pointed out the heterogeneity of these people and their concerns. The fact is that these were few; even fewer were those who went beyond these readings that, despite adding nuance to partisan readings and therefore seeking consensus, did not offer a comprehensive understanding of what had taken place. The fact is, when recalling the conflict, we observe how a variety of factors played out, including economic, political, spatial and socio-cultural, that cannot simply be set in the field of ideology or simple mediation. These are indeed factors that require a more comprehensive reading and above all more attention to the political economy of space and the functioning that ideology can have when it comes to blurring the importance it has in all this. Let's analyze them.

NOTES

1. This chapter is based mainly on the chronology made by Oró Badia (2004), contrasted and complemented with other sources, among which are: a special program on Radio de Premià de Mar (municipal radio), entitled *Crònica d'una mesquita* [Chronicle of a Mosque], a journalistic documentary made by the present author of the Gómez-Fontanills Archive (AGF); a significant number of press clippings provided by Alberto López Bargados; interviews, both formal and informal, carried out during fieldwork; the report of the Gabinet d' Estudis Socials (GES 2002); the study of Jordi Moreras (2009); and finally, the viewing of the documentary *Una mesquita a Premià* [A Mosque for Premià], a documentary produced by TV3 (Television of Catalonia).

2. According to one of my informants, Salama, they previously had a store in Barri Cotet. In fact, she had participated in the activities of the place when she was a child. Now she lives in Barcelona, is 31 years old and works for an NGO. Her parents still live in Barri Cotet.

3. I follow the name that appears in Prado (2008), although in the Special Plan (1997) for Joan Prim Street Nos. 121–123, the name of the Islamic Cultural Center appears as the Alttauba Mosque.

4. Josep Torrents i Morales was first elected mayor in the period directly after the Franco regime, from 1979–1983, as a member of the Esquerra Republicana de Catalunya (ERC), the Republican Left of Catalonia, Catalan pro-independence social-democratic party. But during his second mandate, from 1987–1991, he ran for the local political formation Nova Opció Premianenca. Finally, from 1991–1995, he was a member of Convergència i Unió (CiU)—Convergence and Union, a Catalan nationalist electoral alliance in that lasted from 1978 to 2015. It was a federation of two parties, the larger Democratic Convergence of Catalonia (CDC), a more traditional liberal-center party, and its smaller counterpart, the Democratic Union of Catalonia (UDC), a more conservative Christian democratic party.

5. In an article from 1997 it is recorded that 56 neighbors lived in the building in question. In spite of everything, nowhere does it state the number or percentage of participation of these neighbors in the litigation, nor if the signatories were limited to residents of the same block where the oratory was located.

6. Partit dels Socialistes de Catalunya—Socialists' Party of Catalonia. A social-democratic political party and the Catalan instance of the Spanish Socialist Workers' Party (PSOE).

7. This and the following translations, unless otherwise stated, are by the author.

8. See for instance Broll (2020) and Bosch, Carnero, and Farré (2015).

9. SSTT1 / UO0120 / CERTIF97 / 60, certified by Jordi A. Gonzalez Gutierrez, Secretari Acctal. of the Premià de Mar Town Council.

10. I have found all the urban planning documents either at the town hall or at the Register of Urban Planning of Catalonia (RPUC): http://ptop.gencat.net/rpucportal/

11. *Jumping scale* is a concept that Neil Smith (1993) proposed to conceive and explain the process or strategy by which some political or social actor tries to favor their position and positioning through a change in scale. The most important thing here is that the objections were no longer limited to the neighbors in the building but

to the neighbors in the whole neighborhood; although this was still a diffuse group and we do not know with certainty who signed the petitions. They could have been from the neighborhood in question, as much as from any other, or even another town.

12. All proposals for the location of the mosque can be seen in Figure 1.4.

13. Two years later, in 1999, an expansion of the church was approved. According to the constructed memory, this had always been the planned action.

14. Therefore, it can be argued that the mistake at the political level was, very naively, to pay attention to these protests; a beginner's mistake that despite its naivety led to a very serious social conflict, the consequences of which are still being healed today (Ariño 2010).

15. This is an important fact because, as will be discussed later, it is the decisions of the different social and political agents, and the changes of scale, that ended up taking a concrete form at the collective and discursive level.

16. In an article published in April 2001 we found the following important information: "Building the new mosque has a cost of more than 50 million, and the entity currently only has 18" (Tarramera 2001).

17. In chapter 4 I will deal with the convergences between these paradigmatic cases within their temporal and discursive contexts.

18. The "internal" diversity is very broad, a fact that is often little recognized by the majority society. For an introduction, albeit brief, see the pedagogical guide that we have published with Descontrol: *Islamofòbia? An educational proposition* (2020).

19. Despite the fact that, as of the year 1992, according to the compilation of Moreras (1999: 178–179), Premià de Mar ceases to be the only oratory between Mataró and Badalona, it is to be assumed that the Muslims who attend are not limited to Premià de Mar.

20. In the Spanish state there was the Spanish Federation of Islamic Religious Entities of Spain (FEERI) and the Union of Islamic Communities of Spain (UCIDE).

21. In the articles written as a result of the closure of the oratory on the ground floor of Verge de Núria Street, the newspapers do not agree on the area of the premises: some say that it was less than 50 m², others that it was 60. Despite this, what is striking are the two articles in *La Razón* and *ABC* published on the 13th of November. They describe significant neglect of important details about the events, sometimes overtly supplemented with false information. See, for example, the following excerpt from *La Razón*: "At the meeting it was also agreed to create a commission to build a new mosque on a site owned by the town council." Apart from this falsehood, the title of the article is "Closing a mosque in Premià after a neighborhood pact" (Editorial Office, *La Razón*, 2001).

22. There is very little information about the role the Consulate played in the matter. It does not appear to have been significant and, in fact, the Consulate does not enter the conflict again.

23. I have tried to access the documentation to find out what the allegations were and with what arguments they were presented, but the town council did not want to provide them.

24. The group originally signed as Plataforma Premià per la Convivència but later decided to change to distinguish themselves from the Plataform for Catalonia.

25. Hygiene (something supposedly scientific and objective) is introduced here as a rhetorical device to give more weight to the argument.

26. AIAT paid €7,000 for the license. Only Catholic churches have a tax exemption.

27. Iniciativa per Catalunya Verds - Initiative for Catalonia Greens. An eco-socialist political party in that lasted from 1987 to 2019.

Chapter 2

The Context: Premià de Mar

Premià de Mar[1] is a coastal town in the Maresme region, the area of which is 2.1 km,[2] and which had 27,802 inhabitants in 2010, giving it a demographic density of 13,239 inhabitants per square kilometer (Idescat 2010). The municipality borders to the east with Vilassar de Mar and to the west with El Masnou, to the north with Premià de Dalt and to the south with the Mediterranean Sea. It is located in the south of the region and lies approximately 20 km from Barcelona, a city with which it is connected by the R1 railway. This stretch of the railroad, the first on the Iberian Peninsula, links Barcelona with the towns of Maresme.

Figure 2.1: Premià within the Maresme region and near Barcelona.
Source: Catalan Institute of Cartography and Geoinformation (ICGC) (2010).

MIGRATORY MOVEMENTS AND
URBAN TRANSFORMATIONS

If Manuel Delgado's (1997) observation that in the city we are all, in some way, immigrants, is correct, then the truth is that this fact often goes unrecognized. However, if we look at the history of Premià de Mar, immigration has been a continuous phenomenon and from the town's earliest days. Of the 27,545 inhabitants in Premià de Mar in 2008, only 7,090 were born in the Maresme region, while 17,628 were born elsewhere in Catalonia. In the same way, we see how the population growth during the last 70 years has been the following: 1950–1960 (40 percent), 1960–1970 (105 percent), 1970–1979 (70.5 percent), 1980–1991 (18 percent), 1991–2001 (16 percent) and 2001–2008 (4.6 percent). These data, compiled by the author from Idescat (2010), show that the increase experienced by Premià de Mar in the years 1960–70 was comparatively much more significant than that experienced in the last twenty-five to thirty years.

Over the last thirty years, there have been processes key to understanding the recent history of Premià de Mar and its urban transformation. These include the population shifts at a town level that have possibly gone unnoticed in the statistics and the boom in building semi-detached houses marketed to well-to-do families. In truth, there has been a double immigration, a more visible one and another, which is ignored; a distinction in terms of the social visibility of immigration in Premià de Mar that will become essential for our research. On the one hand, we have an "invisible," or rather, ignored,[2] immigration of upper-middle-class people primarily from Barcelona and the metropolitan area in general.[3] On the other hand, we have much more visible immigration of people from Senegal, Gambia, Morocco and Latin America, primarily workers.

Therefore, it is essential to draw attention to the fact that, in a theoretical sense, due to their mobility, immigrants could also be considered the same as those from the south of Spain (which I will call "former immigrants") and therefore, extra-communitarian. At the same time, the difference that exists at the social level between these two types of mobility must also be underlined, both in the perception of the inhabitants (people do not perceive them as immigrants, a quite stigmatizing term, but as residents, or something similar) and in the treatment and status they enjoy. Because "immigrants" (be they old or new) are visible, mainly due to their "other" way of being and appearing, and for that very reason they are distinguishable, while on the other hand, the other newcomers from close range and the middle class are not.

Yet each of these imagined immigrant communities—in Benedict Anderson's (1993) sense—come to Premià for very different reasons. Some come from the metropolitan area of Barcelona. They come to ride the wave of social mobility through consumption; they may also come in search of another way of living and be open to diversity. Even though they have lived in the town only for a short time, they are generally not considered strangers or outsiders. On the other hand, those considered "immigrants" or "foreigners," come both from both inside and outside the European Union. For example, Romanians come to the region mainly searching for work, their economy being the primary concern as it will secure their living standard. This double standard in the perception of immigrants intrigues me particularly, and even more so its relationship with the town's urban transformation. As we have already seen, the spatial component is vital; after all, the migratory phenomena occur in a specific space, neighborhood, or town. In fact, one of the fundamental ideas of this research is that these two processes, immigration and urban transformation, are deeply related, and, therefore, it is essential to analyze them to understand the case.

PREMIÀ DE MAR: THE FUTURE OF A TOWN

[M]y father worked in the fields, he was a *pagès* [a Catalan peasant farmer]. My mother worked as a babysitter in Mataró, in a house of a very important man, and she was working there all day, making food, making the beds, taking care of the house, right? So when they could, they saved up a little and bought a house here in Premià, in Joan Maragall Street. A small house of those cheap simple houses. Back then, the Premià landscape was dominated by all these factories. The Vapor Vell factory, the chair factory, Can Sanpere, an industrial town of factories, and most of the inhabitants were employed in the factories. So from Gran Via down you had the nucleus of the town, from Gran Via up there, were fields of crops, carnations, potatoes, fields, and only two streets, Joan Maragall Street, and then much further up, near the Verge de la Merced, a small alley where the teachers lived, which is where the houses of the national teachers were located. So the panorama was this, the old town a ghetto, a Catalan stronghold, well people from here, and then the people who were arriving, lived in Joan Maragall, they even called it Calasparra street because many people from Murcia went to live there, and the other street and then Barri Cotet, the rest were fields. Then the great construction era began, and Gran Via upwards was urbanized until it became overcrowded. That is the panorama of Premià that I remember from when I was little, and well, people, more or less lived together, worked in factories (. . .) they never had any common meeting places, no no no, it wasn't in their interest, they came here to work, my parents came here to work, they didn't come to see the *sardanas* [Catalan dance] or to understand the Catalan history. (Pedro, fifty-seven years old and former resident of the Maresme neighborhood)

The town was founded in 1836, then called San Cristóbal de Premiá (Coll 2009). At first, it was a fishing neighborhood segregated from what was then called Sant Pere de Premià (now Premià de Dalt). The main economic activities in the municipality during these early periods were fishing, the textile industry, navigation (the incipient trade with the Americas, which would develop notably throughout the nineteenth century), as well as agriculture, whether it was dry land (vineyard and cereals) or noria (orchard and fruit trees, especially oranges). The construction of the first railway line in Spain, from Barcelona to Mataró (1848), undoubtedly helped the growth of the town (which would double the number of inhabitants in forty years to reach 2,239 in 1900, an upward trend that would continue into the twenty-first century) and its commercial activities in subsequent years. In this sense, the description made by Víctor Balaguer in the *Guide from Barcelona to Arenys de Mar by the Railroad* (1985) is very significant:

> Premiá de Mar or San Cristóbal de Premiá is a town of little importance. It has 1,500 souls and 280 neighbors [heads of household], three textile factories, two for stiffening and one for Pisan, handkerchiefs etc., with their dye, each employing thirty people.
>
> The primary industry of this town, which comprises 400 quarters of land, is navigation. The lands produce wine, wheat, barley, hemp, legumes and onions, and their main harvest is wine, but unfortunately, six years ago, everything was lost because of oidium [a fungus].
>
> Premiá's registration has twelve fishing boats and one cabotage vessel; and other license plates, but assembled by residents of this town as owners and interested parties, there are four of cabotage and ten from the America's Cup . . .

In the following decades, the introduction of steam navigation had managed to diminish the importance of the town's shipping industry. The agricultural sector also suffered greatly from the plague of phylloxera, which obliterated the town's vineyards. Despite this, thanks to growing industrialization from the nineteenth century on, Premià de Mar would grow slowly. Thus, several vital factories were established, including textile, metal, and manufacturing (Can Puiggròs, the Gas Factory, Can Serra Oller), which would later be called Vapor Vell, the Roura Foundry the Lyon Barcelona—a pioneer in Lyonnaise stamping. For this purpose, labor was required and, as explained by Tria (2003, 106), the entrepreneurs chose to bring qualified workers, mainly from the famous textile colonies along the Llobregat and Ter Rivers. To attract these workers, houses were built for their families to live in for the duration of their employment. As a result, people began to arrive from the interior of Catalonia and, later, after the construction of the Barcelona Metro in the twentieth century, many people came from Murcia and the Valencian Community.

These first waves of newcomers to the town meant the first phase of restructuring the urban panorama. A second phase began in the 1950s after the Franco regime imposed economic and political reforms, largely following the proposals later made in the World Bank Report of 1962, also called the First Development Plan. These reforms caused internal migration driven by hunger and poor development in some areas of southern Spain. In fact, 1950–1970 was the period with the highest rates of migratory movements that have even been seen in the municipality of Premià de Mar, as can be seen in the following statistical data: In 1950, 3,947 inhabitants lived in Premià, today they live around of 28,000. Throughout the last sixty years, the total growth has been set out at the beginning of this chapter.[4]

These migrations were dominated by people from Murcia, Extremadura and Andalusia.[5] The newcomers worked in all of the sectors for which the region was known: agriculture, as Maresme had become an important region both in floriculture and in the cultivation of some fruits such as strawberries and parts of the viniculture, Alella; industry; and, above all, construction, notable as one part of the new population would work on the houses of the other part. Entirely new neighborhoods were built, among them Barri Cotet, which stands out for being built mainly by its original inhabitants and because it was not close to the city center as it was isolated in agricultural fields. In Pedro's story, we see these two processes of immigration and settlement reflected through his parents:

> [W]hen my parents arrived they went to live in Vilassar de Mar, and they shared the apartment with another family, a tiny apartment, and there were two families. Of course, when they were both working and making a little money, they bought their own house . . . [First] they lived in Vilassar. It was the typical immigration pattern, right? First came my mother, because she was the one who could, she left after the war . . . She came because a friend who was hiding here during the Franco era was looking for a job in Mataró for her, and she came here. Well, when she found a place, she looked for a job for my father, then when he had a job in the fields, my father came here . . . So my father lived in the countryside in a shack, and my mother lived in the house of "influential men." When they gathered enough money, they rented an apartment in Vilassar de Mar together with a family, friends of theirs. Next thing, my mother brought her mother, the grandmother, so that, since they both work, she could help her around the house. Then I'm born . . . Then my father looked for a house here in Vilassar de Mar . . . He brought his father, and he brought the brothers along, and in the end, the whole family ends up settling down here. (Pedro, fifty-seven years old and former resident of the Maresme neighborhood)

Pedro's story is emblematic since it shows the typical trajectory of many immigrants from the south of the Spanish state and their settlement to the new urban space of Premià de Mar. It was already a space characterized by segregation between the original settlers and the new immigrants; in fact, the Gran Via was, in this sense, the border between the old nucleus and the new extension under construction. From the old agricultural land emerged the multifamily housing blocks of the new Maresme neighborhood, the "grey blocks" (where the first mosque would later be located) in Verge de Núria Street:

> Flats built as speculation, very poorly made, very cheap with lousy material, as is logical, occupied by immigrant people, which was the cheapest they found . . . If you look at them, you can see that they are very poorly made, of inadequate materials. And those who rented them speculated a lot, that's why people got involved, well, the blacks when they lived there, those who lived there and are still living . . . Now notice that, if you walk by and look at them, you realize that they have been renovated on the outside, but there are still problems on the inside. (Pep, sixty-seven years old and resident in the Eixample neighborhood)

At the same time, other blocks were being built near the beach. They were apartment blocks built in the style of the time, in which at first rich people used to spend the summer, as Pep says, "The summer residents were people, let's say 'rich people' who came to take the waters at Premià, recommended in the north of Europe as waters with much iodine and the beaches were known to be very clean." Despite this, little by little, they were staying for longer and eventually became residents.

Thus we see how the aged appearance of the town began to change with the low houses. However, the urban transformation did not stop in the seventies but was changed by several others. For instance, we see how in the eighties, several multi-family housing blocks were built, such as those built by the savings bank La Caixa la Sagrada Familia. Among the people who would live there, many were, as Pep explains:

> [T]he employees of La Caixa "L a Sagrada Familia," were people from Barcelona who had some money in the bank and Mr. Domenech bought them a flat, or maybe they wanted to invest because, of course "we have some coins, what do we do? man, we make some blocks of flats that are very beautiful" . . . Those flats ended up being rented first to summer residents. Then the family, the sons or the daughters came to live there, like many flats in Premià, it was a theoretically well-off people . . . Either they were employees of the same savings bank or they were employees of a company, and they had a little money and the director of the bank or whatever, encouraged them to buy a flat, it's that simple. (Pep, sixty-seven years old and resident in the Eixample neighborhood)

It is at the exact moment that people from the Gambia, Senegal and Morocco began to arrive, primarily men who came to work in the agriculture sector (Jabardo 1999) and later in the construction sector, as Youssef explains:

> In my case, well, I saw another cousin here, and I spoke with the boss of a building company to work with him. I was with him for a year and a half . . . and from then on . . . I had to find another solution because the visa and immigration law was applied, and with this person, he had not been able to give me a pre-contract, so I had to go to another place in Spain where they had offered me a pre-contract. This way, I have been able to legalize, and when the job was finished, I had to look for another opportunity here and . . . I got it about two weeks after arriving. I applied for a position, worked for a workplace here in agriculture, and the manager had already given it to me, and I have now been working there for fourteen years . . . Until I left voluntarily and joined the construction sector, which I have been in for almost six years . . . and here we are. (Youssef, forty-eight years old and resident in the Maresme neighborhood)

Women, who arrived later, in many cases by way of family reunification, would work informally in domestic services, mainly cleaning and taking care of the houses (townhouses, towers, mansions)[6] of the newcomers, the richest of the metropolitan area, who were also arriving at this time. The new immigrants settled in the same areas as the salaried, former-migrant workers from the south: the vast majority in Barri Cotet or the Maresme neighborhood. This is how Salama explains the immigration history of her father:

> [M]y father, well, he came to Premià in the eighties. Before, he had lived in the Basque Country and such . . . He worked in a metallurgical company in the Basque Country and then . . . Well, because of what usually happens, if a relative goes to Premià and says, well, come here because there is more work and so on . . . Well, in the end, he went to Premià, and in the end, they got together; it's a bit like a grouping of the people who were in the town in Morocco because they are the same ones . . . So the people who were here at the beginning were acquaintances, neighbors, etc., in Doctor Flemming Street, and finally in Barri Cotet, where my parents bought a house. (Salama, thirty-one years old and former resident of Barri Cotet)

This way, entering the 1990s, we find a town that takes the shape we see it today.

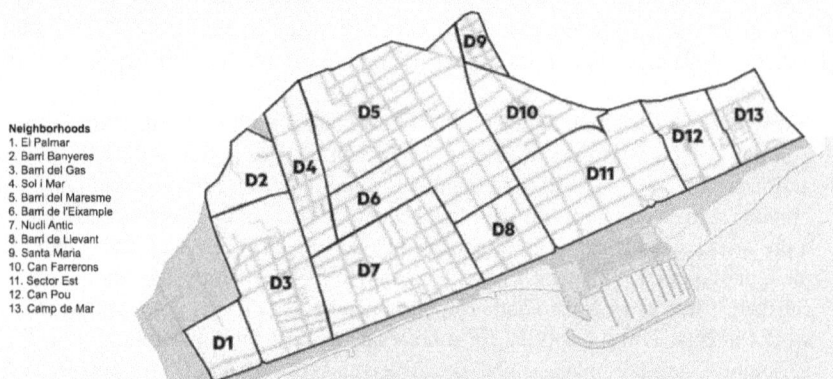

Neighborhoods
1. El Palmar
2. Barri Banyeres
3. Barri del Gas
4. Sol i Mar
5. Barri del Maresme
6. Barri de l'Eixample
7. Nucli Antic
8. Barri de Llevant
9. Santa Maria
10. Can Farrerons
11. Sector Est
12. Can Pou
13. Camp de Mar

Figure 2.2: The neighborhoods.
Source: Author's own elaboration from ERC Premià de Mar (2021).

TODAY'S PREMIÀ DE MAR

Premià de Mar today comprises a very compact population center, formally made up of twelve neighborhoods, as shown on the following map (see figure 2.2).

These neighborhoods, at a general level, vary significantly in social, human and urban terms, and that could be classified into three types, which also correspond more or less with their historical appearance as we have seen it described so far: (1) a heritage zone dominated by low-rise houses where the "oldest" inhabitants and others with a high cultural capital mainly reside, coming from Barcelona and other nearby municipalities, such as Casc Antic and Masia Ribes; (2) areas dominated by multi-family dwellings built in the period of the 1960–1980s, where the majority of migrant workers, from Spain and abroad, reside, including Maresme, Eixample and Cotet (also known as the Barri Santa Maria); and (3) areas of new construction from the period of the 1980s until well into the twenty-first century, where low-rise, single-family and large buildings predominate, and where the majority of upper-middle-class inhabitants reside who came in their retirement. They came mainly from the adjacent municipalities and Barcelona, including El Palmar, Barri del Gas, Banyeres, Sol i Mar, Sector Est, Can Pou and Camp de Mar. Here I will focus on the first two categories.

The properties in the town closest to the sea are stately, large, with very high doors of robust wood.[7] Mixed in with these are modest blocks of flats and houses with significant historical and cultural value. This Casc Antic, as the inhabitants call it, is surrounded by factories, a few still in operation while others have been converted into a school, a museum or houses. Upwards and west, towards the interior, the Gran Via, a commercial street that separates the oldest part of the city from the newer in the north, runs parallel to the beach. This new part approaches the city limits on both sides and is formed mainly by residential areas with towers, landscaped gardens, and mansions.

Although the town can be described at a general level as a bedroom town, the fact is that some neighborhoods are livelier than others, such as Maresme, Barri Cotet and the town center. Maresme and Barri Cotet are the most populated areas, and when you look at them, the first thing that jumps out is the predominance of tall buildings and blocks. In addition, they have a somewhat more degraded appearance than the other neighborhoods, that is, the infrastructure (streets, buildings, squares, etc.) is generally less well-cared for and sometimes even unavailable.

In fact, the neighborhoods of Maresme and Barri Cotet were founded by immigrants from southern Spain during the period of the 50–70s, and the houses were either self-built (as in the case of Barri Cotet) or were built for newcomers or those expected to come. At these early phases, the inequalities still present today were seeded. According to some residents, the Gran Via did not just bisect the town. The road created a social division:

> Gran Via downwards, which they [now] call Casc Antic, are more or less Catalan people, old families from the town . . . And Gran Via upwards, the extensive construction of the 50s, 60s–70s, is where all the immigration from Murcia, Extremadura, other parts of Spain concentrated. (Pedro, fifty-seven years old and former resident of the Maresme neighborhood)

What was previously known as "Gran Via upwards" comprises today's Maresme, the Eixample and Barri Cotet. Populated by immigrants from the south or other parts of Spain (to Premià especially from Murcia), the socio-geographical separation has an analogue in the sociolinguistic separation between "the Spanish" or "Xarnegos," and "the Catalans" or those of *pura cepa* (pure bred).

In this sense, it is significant that today one of the characteristics of these neighborhoods is a large number of older people, the vast majority of whom came from the south. However, we also know, according to the statistical data of the report presented by Pascual and Sánchez (2005), that Maresme and Barri Cotet are the neighborhoods where the percentage of "new immigrants" is higher (16.82 percent and 21 percent of the total inhabitants in the two neighborhoods, respectively). At the town level, most of them live in Maresme, and in some sections of the neighborhood they represent 20–30 percent. Among these, people with Moroccan, Senegalese and Gambian nationality predominate. In addition, I found that in Maresme, where most of this fieldwork was conducted, there are imported food businesses, mainly from African countries, and phone booths, two types of business traditionally associated with immigration from outside the European Union.

With this brief presentation, we close the introduction to the context of this research. The next chapter will scrutinize this context that presents itself socially and culturally as something natural and inevitable, and we will show the opposite: the town's appearance and population distribution are due to factors that are constructed rather than organic. It is clear that spatial planning has something of a contingent, but as we will see in the next chapter, specific economic and political interests also end up driving certain changes and conflicts over others.

NOTES

1. Often people only say Premià, which, in principle, could point to the fact that there is no distinction between the town on the coast, Premià de Mar, and the town further inland, Premià de Dalt, although I have not been able to verify it. Be that as it may, it must be emphasized that the people of Premià de Mar with whom I have been able to speak make a distinction, and this is surely due to the differences at a social level, facilities and spaces between one municipality and another.

2. Pascual and Sánchez (2005, 47) observe that other immigrations seem to go more unnoticed, and that people tend to speak mainly of Moroccans, Senegalese or Gambians, when referring to migratory movements.

3. In the intra-state migratory balances we can see how in 1988 there was a positive balance of people mostly from the same province (422 people), and in the following years they are: 297 (1989), 428 (1990), 129 (1991), 36 (1992), 172 (1993),-62 (1994), 3 (1995), and 123 (1996). From 1996 to 2008 it is negative, but if we look only at the people who enter from the same province, we see that they are stable, although at the end of the 1990s there is a slight increase: 699 (1997), 685 (1998), 655 (1999), 673 (2000), 519 (2001), 564 (2002), 791 (2003), 626 (2004), 696 (2005), 651 (2006). Thus, precisely at the time of the conflict there seems to be a decline. Source: Idescat (2010).

4. Own elaboration from Idescat (2010).

5. Although migrants from other autonomous communities of the Spanish state continued to arrive in Catalonia, the truth is that the same attention is not usually paid to people from outside the state.

6. A trend that has only been consolidated over the years, with some differences such as that many had to look for work outside the city. Thus, after the saturation of construction in Premià de Mar, and even earlier, many men work in the same construction sector in other towns of the Maresme, such as Premià de Dalt, or in the agricultural holdings of Vilassar de Mar. In the same way there are also many women who work in the service sector in Premià de Dalt, Vilassar de Dalt or Alella.

7. As Tria (2003, 106) explains, these are the old houses of "the sailors," captains of freight ships.

Chapter 3

Premià de Mar within the Geography of Capitalism

The main argument on which this research rests is that any analysis of a conflict over or in space, such as conflicts over mosques, must include analytical attention to the spatial logic. To this end, I have applied a perspective from the political economy of space, starting from the theory of the production of space developed by Henri Lefebvre (1991). The basic idea that Lefebvre advocates, which follows the ideas of Marx (2008), is that space is the continuous result, always unfinished and dynamic, of a dialectical relationship between the human being, immersed in social relations, and their environment (Harvey, 2001; Martínez Veiga, 1991; Narotzky, 2005). This directly contradicts the Euclidean idea of space,[1] according to which space is something neutral, an empty context, a mere container for "the social."

The consequence of considering space in this way is that it can be extracted from its social, political, cultural, economic context and treated as a project, a mere residue; in short, it can be annihilated without question. Contrary to this, Lefebvre proposes seeing space as political and strategic. Space, Lefebvre argued, is never neutral but lived in conformity with the fact that it is linked with users in a dialectical relationship. Furthermore, he adds, it is linked to the reproduction of social relations, so that space is not "a scientific object misguided by ideology or politics; it has always been political and strategic" (Lefebvre 1976, 46). In fact, Lefebvre continues, space has a paradoxical character, because it is double faceted: "it is immediate and mediate, that is, it belongs to a certain near order, the order of adjacency, and to a more distant order, society, the State." (Lefebvre 1976, 38).

Following this line of argument and that of Franquesa (2007), I propose investigating the spatial logic of the geography of capital, that is, the spatial logic of capitalism. Although the logic of capitalism in the background pretends that space fulfils two functions simultaneously, the function of means of production and product. In other words, in the geography of capitalism, space tends to have two primary functions: on the one hand, it would be an effect, a commodity, and on the other hand, a resource for "economic processes that have as their object the production of surplus-value and the reproduction of society in order to guarantee this accumulation process" (Franquesa 2007, 127). These two purposes are varied, and there may be conflicts of interest between how it is used as a commodity and as a tool for commercial purposes. In addition, there tends to be a conflict between the mercantile purposes and the social purposes of space because although space can be a means of production and product (merchandise), it would also serve as merchandise in the consumption process and as a means of reproduction. This type of conflict is nothing more than a manifestation of the contradiction between use-value and exchange-value described and analyzed by Marx (2008).

According to Marx, within the commodities of capitalist production, we find a dialectic between use values and exchange values. The use-value of an object lies in its usefulness and social significance, which is directly linked to its materiality and consumption. While use-value is not unique to the capitalist economic system, exchange value is. Moreover, it is fundamental for Marx's theory: although use-value is the material support for exchange value, "as use-values, commodities are, above all, different in quality; as exchange-values, they can only differ by their quantity, and therefore do not contain a single atom of use-value" (Marx 2008, 46).

The exchange value results from the work invested in the merchandise to exchange it. In such a way that, to accumulate money through the exchange, the space must necessarily be measurable or quantifiable, and to measure it, space must be neutral, empty. That is, the capitalist system tends to produce a measurable space through the fragmentation of the land into private property, which thereby becomes a commodity.

Despite this, the idea of space as the merchandise is fallacious (Polanyi 2001, 71–80) because both space (the earth), money and man, are what Karl Polanyi called fictitious merchandise since they are elements without which life cannot be conceptualized and from which to separate life would be a fiction. Therefore, to maintain this fiction of a commodity, one must continually separate space from life through abstraction. Given the nature of capitalism, a particular space has to be produced: a space that can be sold, consumed, or function as a means of production. Alternatively, given the nature of space, capitalism needs a (re)presentation of space as something neutral, passive and static, the product of technical human actions on it, e.g., of technocrats, architects, or urban planners. This is a practice that I will call urbanism following Franquesa (2005, 60) and Debord (1995).

This urbanism has a neoliberal variant (neoliberal urbanism), characterized by an intensification of the work of adapting to the demands of the capitalist accumulation system. Thus, under neoliberal capitalism, urban-political regulations play a fundamental role (Brenner and Theodore 2002): their primary purpose is to pursue and implement the optimal conditions to extract surplus value. In other words, capitalism in its neoliberal variant depends on the State as a kind of mediator: the creator and dealer of the land (Lefebvre 1976; Weber 2002, 523–4) but also as the apparatus that ensures control and reproduction (Gupta and Ferguson 1997). It is, however, precisely this idea of a fragile (local) city as an intermediary in a robust (global) economy that gives more power to this economy itself, masking the vital role played by the State (or the administrations) in the deployment of capitalism as shown by Franquesa (2007) in her approach to the concept of gentrification.[2] This is precisely the reason for including urban plans in the analysis of this research.

The evident conclusion of the preceding paragraphs is that there are conflicts between the different users, uses, and purposes of space, that is, conflicts between different economic and political interests of the different social actors in and on a specific space,[3] that is, context historical-geographical. Furthermore, since "society does not obey a logic (. . .) it tends towards it. This society does not represent a system; it strives to be one" (Lefebvre 1976, 42). Therefore, it can be expected that there will be contradictions in space and on space, between different groupings, mainly because there is still a relationship between the production of things and that of space. The argument centers on the production of social relations and reproduction of specific relations of domination, which clarifies why it is crucial to dominate space. We can thus conclude that space is an intrinsic element of society 's production relations and not just a means of production.

For this reason, as an initial and fundamental idea, I take it for granted that space is socially constructed, that is that space is in a dialectical relationship between the different social actors that live in it and the capitalism that structures it. It is a means of production and a product, an ideal process mediated by territorial policies. Consequently, given that the production of space is never fulfilled or homogeneous, although capitalist geography does tend to make it seem like this, conflicts arise between the interests of the different social actors over the concrete space and between the different capitalist actors who want to extract a particular value from the space. From this, we can conclude that there must be contradictions over and in space due to conflicting political and social interests, which leads to the following statement: different interests are being weighed against each other, and these can either diverge or converge.

Finally, I consider it necessary to underline that the processes described so far are not abstract processes carried out by an invisible dwarf, to paraphrase Walter Benjamin, or an invisible hand, as Adam Smith said. Instead, they need physical persons, actors in the system or institutions that carry them out, as well as discourses and narratives that justify their hegemony, such as conceiving that abstract global processes are decisive and that little can be done to avoid them. The actors could be a cultural bourgeoisie, as Martínez Veiga (1991) demonstrated in the case of the transformation of the center of Madrid, upper-middle-class people in the case of Palma de Mallorca (Franquesa 2005) or simply city planners or builders. Regarding justifying discourses and narratives, nowadays, you can continuously hear arguments from private-sector companies and governments about the inevitability of some economic or political processes. The well-worn phrases "there is nothing to be done" or "it 's because of the crisis" must be answers everyone has heard. Often, as Sennett (2006) and Bourdieu (1999) have shown, they are arguments that serve the powerful, irrefutable arguments (determinants) to be able to carry out unpopular actions without protest or resistance. The truth is that they are part of the framework, and not offering the existing alternative readings is collaborating with the ongoing project that is presented as inevitable, even though it may be the best of a set of poor choices. Be that as it may, in the following sections, we will try to describe and analyze the urban planning and transformation processes in Premià de Mar.

THE PLANNING OF THE TERRITORY

The roots of territorial planning in Catalonia go back, according to Majoral et al. (2002), to the middle of the nineteenth century with the consolidation of Barcelona as a great industrial city. Barcelona was beginning to be perceived as the engine of Catalonia and "the point of origin of a dynamism that benefited the whole of the country and the main backbone of the Catalan territory" (Majoral et al. 2002, 403). The history of planning in the region can be distilled into five stages. During the nineteenth century, there was urban expansion and the creation of the bourgeois city. Then, during the first third of the twentieth century, there was the work of the Commonwealth and the plans of the Republican Generalitat. The third stage came in the post-civil war, with the Barcelona Metropolitan area and the Franco regime. After which comes the fourth phase with the territorial debate of the years of political transition, followed by today 's fifth phase, beginning with the General Territorial Plan of Catalonia (PTGC). Here I will limit myself to the latter.

The PTGC was approved in 1995 by the Generalitat de Catalunya. Until then, most of the sectoral plans were already being carried out, such as the General Plans of Ordination (PGO), but the PTGC would be conceived as the general framework of reference for future actions in the territory. In the PTGC proposal, we see how the southern part of the Maresme region is located within a regional system classified as being a "system of expansion and articulation of the central system of the metropolitan area," which still has the capacity for spatial growth (PTGC, M. 98).

Even though according to the Catalan Autonomous Statute of 1979, the Parliament of Catalonia has exclusive powers in terms of urban planning and spatial planning, most of the urban planning carried out in Catalonia in recent decades derive from the actual contents of the 1959 Land Law and the revisions in 1976, 1990 and 1992 (Majoral et al. 2002, 420). Contrary to the established position that the initiative, development, and execution of urban planning is, according to current legislation (2001), a municipal competence, the final content must be approved by higher authorities, in this case, the Government of the Generalitat.

> The law also establishes two basic types of planning: general and derivative. General planning covers the whole of a municipal term and includes three basic types, depending on the level of detail with which the municipal territory is planned and the land uses are delimited. These are the General Urban Planning Plans (PGOU), the Subsidiary Planning Standards (NNSS) and the Urban Land Delimitation Projects (PDS). The derived planning comprises three types (partial plans, special plans, and detailed studies), whose function it is to develop the planning of a part or a specific sector of the municipality. (Majoral et al. 2002, 420)

The General Urban Plans are the most complete as they design a complete model of future growth of the municipal territory, and their elaboration requires an interdisciplinary technical team (architects, economists, lawyers, geographers, sociologists, biologists).

In 1991, the Premià de Mar Municipal General Urban Plan (PGMOU-PM) was finally approved. The plan was drawn up by the architects Limón-Ruiz Valles. At a general level, it has three Subsidiary Regulations (NNSS), a Partial Plan (PP), six Special Plans (PE) and eleven Detailed Studies (ED), among which the "La Lionesa" sector and the "La Salle" sector were already directly resolved by the PGO. In its essence, it constitutes a modification to another General Management Plan (PGO) previously proposed.[4] This modification was because the old PGO, the PGO del Maresme Sur (definitively approved in 1963 and later supplemented with the Landscape and Tourism Regulations in 1966), had become obsolete. According to the report, it was based on the old land law of 1956, which in the meantime had been repealed and replaced with a new act of the same title in 1975. Thus, the new general plan (PGMOU-PM—for ease, I shall call it PGO-91) resulted from a review and adaptation of the new land law of 1975 and the current regional law on the adaptation measures the urban planning of Catalonia (3/1984 of January 9). The latter was a modification of the PGO del Maresme Sur (1963), converting the Regional Plan of the sub-region "Maresme Sur" into new PGOUs, consisting of the nine municipalities of Alella, El Masnou, Cabrera, Cabrils, Premià de Mar, Vilassar de Dalt, Premià de Dalt, Teià, and Vilassar de Mar (PGO-91, 1002).

The PGO-91 of Premià de Mar is vital because any subsequent modification has to be made from this referential framework that constitutes the general plan until the approval of the POUM 2008. Furthermore, it already contained special plans and units of action that would later be carried out. By assessing the planning model, we can conclude that the town planners wanted to promote a particular type of immobilization or fixation[5]: they wanted to ensure that the young people (children of the inhabitants of that time) stayed in the area into adulthood. To this end, there was an emphasis on enhancing semi-detached homes of a mid-range value. They also wanted to convert second homes into primary residences in order, as they said, to energize the city and start an integration process.

In this case, the central axis of the plans, the migratory movements that they want to "capture," are people with high purchasing power. An example is given in the following sentence of point c): "[A] meticulous urban design with a unique character capable of offering an alternative aspect to the suburban character that the extension of the town has recently acquired." (PGO-91, 1050). It is never explicitly stated, but if we examine the criteria to be followed when constructing new houses, it seems evident that they cannot be blocks of flats. Some guidelines include 1) the constructions of low buildings (with regard for their overall height), 2) no building or changing the use of city-garden areas, and 3) possible de-densification.

On its face, PGO-91 goes against the "chaotic urbanism"; an urban development that, according to the planners, took root in the 1960s and 1970s where open spaces and coherent arrangements were not taken into consideration. In Premià at the time, mainly inspired by the actions of Josep Maria de Porcioles Colomer in Barcelona, the mayors allowed the Eixample areas to be built up intensively. Based on statements from my informants, I have been able to discern that Premià de Mar had no formal municipal plan until then. The only scheme had been to cater to the needs of the large landowners and speculative construction; the land was merely a product to exploit. The new plan would partly solve some of these problems, but it would also give rise to another type of urban planning (in the end, it even contemplated the complete urbanization of Premià de Mar), this time perhaps not so wild but decisive for the city, and particularly the Maresme neighborhood.

A NEIGHBORHOOD DESTROYED AND REVALUED

The different urban plans outlined in the previous section are the tools through which, ideally, one space or another is produced. Therefore, we must investigate the urban plans carried out on the Maresme neighborhood based on the PGO-91.

When considering each of the plans that have had material effects on the Maresme neighborhood, it is striking that they try to promote the construction of single-family homes within the expansion, in addition to reinforcing city-garden areas, where, according to the PGO-91 zoning, multi-family housing cannot be built. They also try to promote public squares, the purpose of which, they say later, would be to sponge the area to facilitate subsequent private investment, since, without it, no developer wanted to invest in the area; parking spaces; and multi-family homes, which will turn out to be of a high standard.

If the PGO-91 indeed has a regional dimension, we must look at other actions that have been carried out from the municipal level to trace it. These actions involve: 1) planning an industrial area in the periphery; 2) the renovation and interior reforms of the old town; and 3) the construction of a marina. Although indeed, the PGO-91 had already laid the foundations for this development, these new plans and modifications made later have been decisive for the new space. We will see below from a detailed analysis of two paradigmatic development interventions in the Maresme neighborhood.

Frigoríficos del Maresme SA, from Frozen Food to a Quiet Environment

A modification of the PGO-91 of 1996 (DUN File 1995/000404/B) summarizes a significant problem that is quite interesting for this study. In what is called an "island of houses" delimited by the streets of Montserrat, Elisenda de Moncada, Pilar, and Joan Prim, we find a factory that has been in use for more than 35 years. There is not much information about the factory; the only certainties are that it dates from the late 1950s and early 1960s, the name of the company was Frigoríficos del Maresme SA, and the facility was a distribution center for refrigerated foods. According to PGO-91, any use except residential is permitted on the ground floor where the factory is located. However, with the 1996 modification, it was decided to demolish the factory and change classification for permitted ground floor development. According to the plan, this change lies in the fact that it was estimated that after taking care of the changes produced in the area, there was no longer room for a factory and because there had been unspecified complaints from neighbors.

Anecdotally, however, the evidence points to the fact that the contiguous area had become much more densely populated (according to the team drafting the plan, more has been built than was foreseen in the PGO-91); there are traffic problems through a poorly planned section of the road network where the streets are narrow, there is little space for parking, the trucks that enter and leave and the activities of the workshops in front all of which cause congestion; and finally, there have been complaints about potential traffic that commercial activities could cause, as well as the noise that, according to the neighbors, the machinery produced at night, especially in summer.

According to the urban planning team, adjusting traffic flows would not solve the problem adequately, and as a result, it was proposed to move the factory and rezone the land from industrial usage to urban development. Several proposals were put forward where part of the building would be preserved, but in the end, they chose to demolish the factory facilities that, as they recognized in the same report, "are solid constructions with a complex structure" that was "remarkable on the surface (about 5,000 m² of floor space, excluding basements) and that have not come to the end of their useful life." So, they wanted to renovate the buildings on the island to provide a new residence with a total of 128 homes of medium size of 87 m² and plenty of green space. This "green space" is today a square with hardly any green, and in the surroundings, we no longer find the workshops on Calle Pilar; many have simply been converted into flats. On the other side, the one facing Calle de Montserrat, we have semi-detached houses with private gardens today.

The plan was the first outlining expansion and a transformation of the neighborhood from industrial to residential, two factors that, in my opinion, show that there was a desire to make the area more peaceful and beautiful. The shift to making neighborhoods beautiful followed an overall trend that was at play during the same period in other urban areas that had, until that point, been mainly industrial. The town was changing in character: the prevailing use became residential and tourist-friendly following the productive base changes. From being a town based mainly on industrial production, it transformed into a residential and services space. The third sector, the services sector, began to dominate, and as Mingione (1981) pointed out, this followed the general trend in industrialized countries in the 1980s. Space began to be produced as a commodity for final consumption rather than as productive.

Now, if we observe the phenomenon on a larger scale, at the level of the metropolitan area of Barcelona, we see that the ideas of the General Territorial Plan of Catalonia are being carried out: factories do not disappear, but are moved, for example to Vallès. Thus, places of production are separated from places of consumption, a known spatial differentiation within capitalism, a specific socio-spatial organization, which is part of a phenomenon that some authors have called post-Fordist or, in the case of the British anthropologist

David Harvey (1990), *flexible accumulation*. We find that local and State administrations in general are beginning to have fewer resources because of a new trend in economic policies at the state and European levels. A situation that delegates to them a certain degree of autonomy in social policies and urban planning. These two factors induce what Harvey (2001) calls the "entrepreneurial turn," where city councils and local governments see in the promotion of the city an economic strategy to finance their policies beyond their limited budgets. Although this is a process that has mainly been observed in large cities, we see through the case of Premià de Mar how it is also a reality for smaller cities and towns, something that other authors have already argued (Vaccaro and Bertrán 2007).

The process at the town level, as observed through the execution of the town plans, is best described by the concept of creative destruction, coined by Joseph Schumpeter (1994) and developed by Jaume Franquesa, following the interpretation of David Harvey, as follows:

> This term defines the insatiable need of capitalism to create new opportunities for surplus-value and, applied to space, designates the incessant labor by which places are simultaneously destroyed and created (devalued and revalued) to obtain benefits. In other words, in order to achieve substantial value differentials, that is, possibilities of solid capital gains, processes that destroy value are required to create the profit opportunity through its revaluation. (Franquesa 2007, 128)

With the destruction of the factory, a new space is created on the island, and the adjacent land and the area, in general, are revalued (in this example, mainly the southern and eastern part of the Maresme neighborhood), and a more homogeneous space is created at the residential level.

However, before the destruction and re-building, the intervention in the place must first be legitimized. As I have already mentioned, these processes are not carried out through a purely commercial production, but the help of the town council is required, giving the changes the imprimatur of the government. The process is not simply and purely economic. Instead, recurring to Rachel Weber 's (2002) observations, an intervention by local administrations is necessary, in addition to requiring a symbolic mobilization of the place to be produced. In other words: the creative destruction of space (hence the production of a different space) requires discourses that dress it up, i.e., discursive practices "by which value is added or subtracted from a certain place" (Franquesa 2007, 129), and which, following Franquesa, I will call *legitimizing narratives*.

Can Tarter: Temporary Free Parking in the Maresme Neighborhood

Hidden behind walls of shrubs, plants, and trees is the Can Tarter farmhouse. Like a green box in the middle of Mercè Rodoreda Square, it is a vestige of earlier times when the area was still fields before it was converted into a temporary parking lot. Cultivating the land had become an unprofitable activity, at least compared to what building could offer. Moreover, with the PGO-91, it had already been decided that the area would have to be changed: parking spaces and more open space were needed. Six years later, in 1997, a Special Urban Renewal Plan for the sector was launched called Tarter-Fornells (UA-9).

According to this plan, the area had a low urbanisation and construction level, thus requiring development. The objectives of the plan were the following: a) find solutions to the dividing walls; b) build "public spaces," such as squares or green areas; c) provide the area with greater parking possibilities; and d) link the existing road network by building new roads. Now, since the fields were already used as parking, it could be argued that they did not need parking spaces or open space per se, but what they wanted was to order the space and the area, empty them and revalue them. In fact, it is striking that no developer had yet been convinced to invest in the area, despite the planned construction of houses, an underground car park, and a hard plaza above it.

In any case, the plan received approval from the Barcelona Urban Planning Commission (CUB) on June 18, 1997, and half a year later, an article in the press explained that the construction company Yonet SA conceived the project; a real estate development company that had specialized in housing construction in the outskirts of Barcelona, particularly the regions of Maresme and Baix Llobregat.

According to this article, the project that the governing team and the construction company had agreed on consisted of building two public squares (with underground parking) and buildings around them. The squares would be built to "mitigate the effects of the wild urbanism of the sixties and seventies," and another objective is added, "to tidy the space, rearrange it and gain public spaces to be able to build community facilities and hold public events." The article's authors describe the Maresme neighborhood as "one of the most degraded areas of the city."

The proposed remodelling would be in three phases. The first one, where four of the seven buildings planned in the southern part of the area would be built, on Montserrat Street,[6] the road network would be fixed and street lighting installed. In the second phase, two apartment buildings and a small square were constructed. Finally, in the last phase, a second plaza and other buildings would be built. Half a year later, some notices were circulated which announced the residential project called Can Tarter. It included the buildings in the northern part of the area; the other buildings in the south were summarily dropped from the project.

In analyzing the urban project underway, especially its social implications, it is quite interesting to analyze a promotional brochure that dates to 1998 for the information it exposes on the equivalence of the euro and the peseta. Its language is impersonal and distant, directed to someone with little actual knowledge of the region and Premià de Mar. However, the map does not show where Premià is, suggesting the author assumes that the location in Catalonia and Maresme is known. Hence, it is unclear who the intended audience is: people from the city or further afield? The leaflet muddies the waters further: "Can Tarter. To enjoy the sun, nature, and the Mediterranean with the advantages of living in the urban center and excellent transport links with the big city. A-19 highway, Renfe station and bus."

Furthermore, on the other side it continues: "Enjoy the Can Tarter residential complex: A new concept of quality of life in the center of Premià de Mar, 200m from the Gran Via. High-quality houses in a spacious and bright setting, perfectly oriented to the sun with about 4,000m² of green landscaped area."

Several elements of the leaflet require attention: 1) it has been written in Spanish rather than in the regional language of Catalan; 2) the prices of the flats are set in euros at a time when the currency was not yet in general use;

Figure 3.1: Brochure.
Source: Unknown Promotor.

3) there is talk of a "new neighborhood"; 4) much emphasis is placed on the central location; 5) the name of the farmhouse is adopted; 6) the language is ambiguous. Through the brochure, they are trying to sell "a new concept of quality of life"; that is, progress and confidence in it, as stated: "High-quality homes in a spacious and bright locale, perfectly oriented to the sun with close to 4,000 m^2 of green landscaped area." Therefore, and although the language might be typical real estate jargon, considered in their totality, these elements suggest that the recipients of this idea would be people from the neighborhood and the town, or neighboring towns, sectors of the working class and immigrants from southern Spain who have been able or who wish to progress socially.

David Prytherch describes the sale of social progress and buying into the future consumption of development concerning urban projects in the Valencian Community. In fact, as a justification for the urban mega-projects there, where it is expected that the agricultural productive base will be destroyed and later replaced by cement and steel, Prytherch (2001) writes of the legitimization of progress and modernity in a place where urban sprawl is taking over even productive agricultural land: "The discourses of modernity have an undeniable structuring force in the debates about Valencia and its urban future . . . We have thus arrived at a polarized discourse, where there is only room for two things: the modern and the non-modern."

An article in *Premià Actual* from October 1998 shows the same narrative logic: in a return to the language of cleanliness, the neighbor was characterized as degraded, and thus it needed tidying, and the spaces rearranged. In this article, the previously sanctioned "wild urbanism" is used to justify redevelopment. There is also the introduction of heritage and historical elements, although they are discussed in terms of value to the environment, which questions the true purpose of their use in the narrative.

Under a heading extolling the cleansing of the area, the article reads: "Keeping the historic Tarter-Fornells farmhouse and the central axis." On the same page, another article contains a quote from the architect of the planning office: "Montserrat Street will be an important area, much like Gran Via, when the planned actions are carried out." This language, taken together with the juxtaposition of the two articles and the accompanying image, I would suggest that the page looks more like advertising disguised as information. For sale is a new neighborhood, a renovation, a new center, but with chosen heritage elements like the farmhouse. For sale is an urban renewal and the revaluation of space, and it is not for sale to all.

We see in this narrative how, through stigmatizing the neighborhood as a justification for intervention, the value of the land has been lowered to destroy it and recreate it to increase its value. The space as a representation holds ideas of progress and heritage as a kind of enchantment. We have been able to see how, through stigmatizing narratives that have served as justification for the interventions, they have tried to lower the value of the land, destroy it, and then promote good evaluations of the new space produced. This represented space contains elements of both an idea of progress and the idea of heritage and the value of historical-cultural elements as a praising factor. In reality, it is as if these cultural elements function as a kind of enchantment, and in fact, they are undoubtedly part of a reconstitution of the neighbourhood 's image, which has now been well-dressed, tidied up and thus ready for sale). The final blow to the old neighborhood comes with the name change: it is still Maresme in the article, but in the press release from the construction company in 1998, the neighborhood is called "Premià."

The Image of a New Neighborhood

A longer-term historical view gives us insight into the neighborhood 's character through its name changes over the last decade. As Pedro says, Maresme did not come to be until the early 1980s when the need for neighborhood associations was raised from "above":

> There was a year, I can't remember when, I think it was when the government of the Socialists [PSC-PSOE], with José Maria Molina, a friend of mine who died recently, that they began to create the neighborhood associations because until then there had been no such thing here. Then they said, to help the city council, because by having more influence in the neighborhoods and capturing the problems there, they began to generate, talk with people so that they could make their association, collect or collaborate, ok? It started then, that should have been around 1984, or around 1983, that 's when the neighborhoods were named. There had never been neighborhoods here, so one day, I found out that I lived in Maresme. How come I live in the neighborhood of Maresme? No, no, now this here is called the Maresme. No, first it was called Barri de les Verges, the Neighborhood of the Virgins . . . Virgen del Pilar, Virgen de Montserrat . . . the Neighborhood of the Virgins. Then some considered that it was no longer the time for this and named it Maresme. (Pedro fifty-seven years old and a former resident in Maresme)

So, as we see, the neighborhood is produced socially and politically. In this case, the construction and the social perception of the inhabitants are subject to a political instrumentalization at the hands of the PSC-PSOE party of Premià de Mar.[7] Thus the neighborhood went from being the Neighborhood of the Virgins (named by the inhabitants) to becoming Maresme (named by the institution). During the mosque conflict, the neighborhood association presented itself as the AAVV of Tarter-Maresme. In the same way, it is very curious that in the meetings of the Coordinator of Neighborhood Associations,

it always appears as AAVV of Can Tarter. Furthermore, today, the neighborhood is officially called the Tarter-Maresme neighborhood.

In this sense, there can be no doubt that this second name change had to do
with the urban transformation in the neighborhood and, perhaps more clearly,
with the Can Tarter urban project. In the end, the name of Tarter-Maresme
is the union of the residential project, Can Tarter, with the name of the old
quarter, Maresme. An informant interprets the changes produced in the
neighborhood:

> Two neighborhoods are born. What was previously a small neighborhood with
> immigrant people from the rest of Spain becomes a neighborhood where these
> original immigrants acquire a different status and constitute, through an urban
> change, a neighborhood of a certain quality. However, that coexists with the rest
> of the neighborhood, now totally degraded and where the [new] immigrants live,
> which is a parallel process . . . Look, they were building the new neighborhood,
> so to speak, [and] each time more African people were moving into the upstairs
> blocks next to the soccer field. (David, forty-eight years old and a resident of
> the Casc Antic)[8]

This production of a new space within the neighborhood entails a new social
segregation between the new workers, immigrants from North Africa, and
the old ones from the south of Spain. To understand more fully how this
socio-spatial segregation happens, it is necessary to add one more observation: this type of segregation can only develop as the new ones replace old
immigrants. In other words, former immigrants can only come to live in the
new Tarter area because new immigrants buy or rent their old homes from
them, often for higher rates than those they replace paid. A similar process has
been observed in many other places in Spain, as Martínez Veiga (1999) has
shown in the case of Roquetas de Mar in Almería, and particularly in other
older neighborhoods in large cities.[9]

This process would be driven mainly by the recent land liberalization
promoted by the Land Law of 1998 (Law 6/1998, on land and the valuation
regime), which produced a real property boom. An interesting effect of the
boom was how the people internalized the mercantile logic to the inhabited
space, and the use-value became exchange-value. The hard-working inhabitants suddenly believed that they could move up the social hierarchy, buy a
bigger home, or simply earn money. Let us see what Pedro, son of Murcian
immigrants, explains on this topic:

> I bought a flat when, well, first, my parents gave me a flat . . . Then when the
> family grew more extensive, we needed more space because it was small. My
> house in 1975 cost me two million and a half pesetas [approx. €15.000], that
> was in 75. In 1985 I bought the second house for four million [€24.000] (I: But

do you change house?) Well, I sold mine and used what I got from it to pay the deposit o the new house, and I signed a mortgage, and I paid the bank for a time, right? The typical history. Then later, about eight years ago, I broke up with my wife, and we decided to sell it. What I bought for four million back then is valued at seventy million pesetas [€420.700], imagine the proportions! . . . So, many people back then bought . . . a lot, and they even bought the apartments in the plans before they were built. (Pedro fifty-seven years old and a former resident of the Maresme neighborhood)

Let us recall that, at this time, the decade of the 90s and the beginning of the twenty-first century, the immigration of people from Morocco and people from Barcelona intensified. The former would settle in the north of the Maresme and Barri Cotet neighborhoods, while the others would be housed in the garden-city areas. There were rumors of overcrowding, mainly in Verge de Núria Street. This is important because, as demonstrated elsewhere,[10] overcrowding (an economic strategy often only used by the first arrivals or in lean times, but always in the short term) no matter how widespread fosters a degrading image of new immigrants.

Therefore, the new immigrants mainly came for work, both in agriculture[11] and the booming construction sector. In order to work, these people needed a place to live, and they ended up establishing themselves where they were allowed to rent or buy, both because of the purchasing power they had and an ethnic segmentation of the market driven by the racism of the owners and renters. Their arrival meant that the supply of flats decreased, and at the same time, with the large new constructions, a new socio-spatial organization was facilitated. Consequently, we can see how a division, an internal segregation, was produced at the level of the Maresme neighborhood. The standard of living of some inhabitants in the south of the neighborhood was improved mainly thanks to the work of the other inhabitants, the immigrant workers. However, as a consequence, they would become a group in opposition, the Others, the new ones to arrive.

At the municipal level, we see that this process essentially has to do with the production of spaces for the consumption of the upper-middle classes (a process that, as I have commented previously, is like gentrification). This process, which also seems to have occurred at the regional level (mainly south of Maresme), had great importance and very marked effects: it involved a remarkable transformation of zones and areas (often old agricultural land) into city-garden zones, such as Can Pou, Camp de Mar, part of the Maresme neighborhood (see the license tables for new first occupations in table 3.1), Banyeres neighborhood and a large part of the historic center.[12]

The target audience of these urban transformations and productions is the middle class of the metropolitan area of Barcelona, whom the developers

Table 3.1. First occupation licenses. Source: Authors own elaboration from municipal data.

Contractor, year	Private, 1999	Yonet SA, 1999 (File 1997 and application 1999)	INPA XXI SA, 2003 (File 19.01.00 & Appl. 21.02.03)	Inmobiliaria Ocean SA, 2000 (File 30.06.97 & Appl. 07.06.00)	Yonet SA, 2000 (File 1998 & Appl. 14.07.00)	Privado, 2001 (File 2000 & Appl. 23.05.01)	Gran Via Uno SL, 2002 (File 2000 & Appl. 01.02.02)
Address	Cisa, 55–60	Mercè, 2–20; Cisa, 5–7; 11–21	Salvador Espriu, 2–20; M. Aurelia Company, 2–24; Joan Vilano, 2–20; Montserrat, 2–10	Joan Prim, 84–86	Montserrat, 22–46	Prim, 8	Prim, 10
Type	5 single-family houses	3 block (104 apartments, 19 stores and 133 parking lots)	31 apartments	28 apartments and 3 stores	Building with 39 apartments and 48 parking lots	Conversion of store into room	Building with 6 apartments

were trying to attract with the idea of living in the towns of Maresme (both those of Dalt and those of Mar) with their tranquillity, proximity to beach and nature (an anti-urban ideal), low population density, cultural authenticity, and so on. The buyers were being sold a specific idea. In fact, the concept of environment is instrumental here in explaining and understanding the process in operation, as Franquesa explains: "An environment is a sum of space-goods which is presented and defined as forming a single whole and sui generis, based on extra-commercial criteria, and based on culture, art, history" (Franquesa 2005, 68). Another attraction may have been the simple fact of climbing the property ladder and gaining in relative social position through the acquisition of a better home; I must emphasize that the vast majority came from living in flats, and now they moved into houses, town-houses or mansions.

The effect was mainly owing to the dramatic rise in house prices in Barcelona, and relatively inexpensive housing in Premià de Mar, although it would change substantially over time. This process, which originated in the 1980s, gave rise to another at the end of the 1990s in the central south of the Maresme neighborhood, a process characterized by the perceived dignity of the neighborhood and by the construction of a new part directed to a seg-ment of the old working population and others coming from the south of the Spanish State, i.e., those who were able to sell their flats and thus fund their new standard of living. This process in turn has another clear effect: it creates a segregation between the new part of the neighborhood and the area that is located above it. The creation and projected affluence of one is built upon the stigmatization of the other.

Amid these processes, the plans for the construction of a mosque appeared. The proposed site on Joan Prim Street is located between two types of residential spaces: the city-garden area and a zone of high rises and small houses (see figures 3.2 and 3.3). Therefore, it is more than plausible that the mosque was read as a threatening, possibly stigmatizing symbol of the cre-ated environment, and therefore, it did not fit within the residents ' logic. In Enric 's words:

> The mosque that they were going to build, the one that was not built, was located at a point that was a limit . . . The houses in front are mansions owned by people with a certain purchasing power, newly built mansions. They are not people who have been living there permanently; they made these mansions in the 1980s or 1990s and . . . I know some people there, from those houses and . . . they fiercely opposed this! Ferocious because it was the mosque in front of their house, and it was like an incredible thing for them, horrible! Moreover, the mosque is in . . . but Joan Prim Street itself is a street that, a little further up the street on the left, are all the streets where most of the black population of Premià lives, but everything would be very close, so of course, no, no . . . That is why it emerged, I understand that that is why the conflict emerged . . . it was an urban conflict from my point of view, an urban conflict, it had nothing to do with, that is, it was affecting the quality . . . in quotes, the quality of life . . . and the prices of the homes there. (Enric, thirty-eight years old and resident of Casc Antic)[13]

Therefore, one might argue that the symbolic expulsion of visible Muslim elements mitigated the threat of a neighborhood of ambivalent character. The residents would attempt to cleanse the image of the neighborhood from pos-sible contamination (Douglas 2002). Thus cleansed and segregated, it would go from being a second-class neighborhood, and with it those who lived there (Punch 2005), to being revitalized, almost first-class street.

Figure 3.2: The height of the buildings in the neighborhood 1997.
Source: Author's own elaboration from Sánchez and Plaza (2021).

Figure 3.3: The height of the buildings in the neighborhood 2021.
Source: Author's own elaboration from Sánchez and Plaza (2021).

Economic interest, I mean because the plot of land where the mosque is, is in an area where only mansions houses can be built, and some of the people who had a mansion around there . . . they sent the message that if the mosque was built the value of the houses would go down . . . The mansion would no longer be worth 100,000 euros; it would be worth 50,000. I call it economic interest . . . , and of course, it is not; on the contrary, since the conflict, the prices have sky-rocketed, they have already more than doubled. (Youssef, forty-eight years old and a resident of the Maresme neighborhood.)

In addition, at the municipal level, it is observed that a negative image had weighed on the town for years and, in particular, the neighborhood. In fact, one day, a resident of Masnou, a forty-something-year-old man, explained to me that he knew people from other neighboring towns who colloquially called him "Premià de Moro" [Premià of the Moors].

There is a contradiction on and in the space of the town between the con-structed images of the place by its various populations and the social lives that take place in them. That is, between a space that immigrant workers, both from Spain and abroad, could inhabit, despite not being in identical conditions, and the production of an ideal space for the consumption of other future inhabitants, people with more purchasing power.[14] Among the most recent urban developments, we can find the renovation of a swimming pool in the Est Sector, the construction of more semi-detached houses in El Palmar and the Est Sector, the Can Farrerons luxury residential project and the expansion of the port. At the same time, contradictions can also be seen between the space as a productive space and a space for mere final, residential consumption.

At a macro level, the town serves as a place for summer recreation or vaca-tions, both for those who have a second residence in the city and those from Barcelona who go to the beach for the day. However, mainly, the city serves as a bedroom city for Barcelona, just like the towns characteristic of the London metropolitan area (PTGC, 30). That is, from the regional administra-tive bodies, such as the regional council, there was an explicit desire to create an area of final consumption for the upper-middle class of Barcelona. It was also a necessity. Even so, despite the outstanding importance that towns of the near periphery, such as Premià de Mar, have had in the socio-spatial organiza-tion of the post-Olympic Barcelona metropolitan area, little study has been done of the role they have played in this. The migratory movements from the center (Barcelona) to the "periphery" (Premià and Maresme in general, which now have their centers), have had vital importance in the restructuring of Barcelona. In the same way that we saw the old immigrants from the south were able to acquire better homes within Premià de Mar thanks to the new immigrants buying or renting their former homes at a profit, and the entire

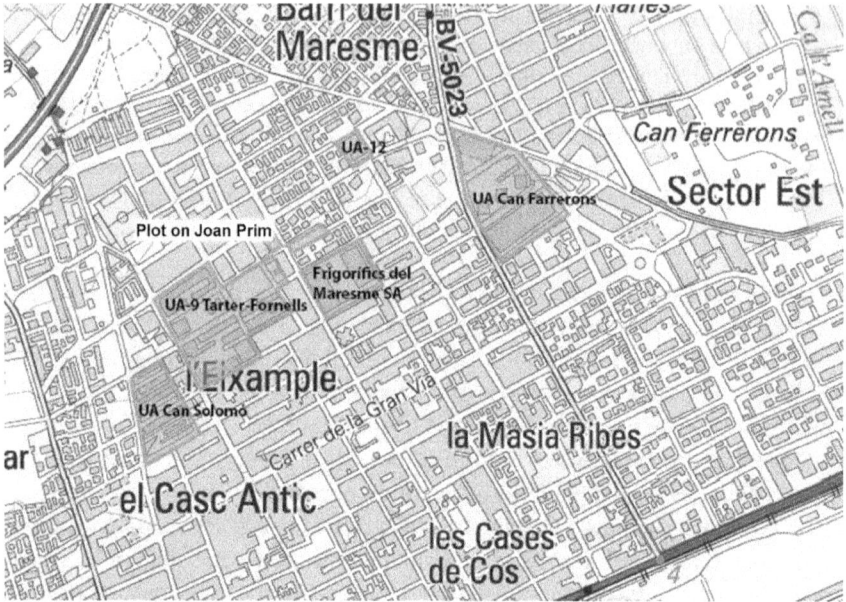

Figure 3.4: Urban actions.
Source: Author's own elaboration from Catalan Institute of Cartography and Geoinformation (ICGC) (2010).

process of related urban transformation, the new arrivals from Barcelona or the 'new residents, 'the old immigrants were able to buy larger, fancier homes and thus acquire a higher level socially speaking, that is, precisely because there were people who acquired their home of origin, revalued; in other words, with an income differential that would allow it to climb socially and economically.

Therefore, in the case of Premià de Mar, we find a true paradox: labor is needed to attract the upper-middle classes of Barcelona and build new houses for the old immigrants. The workers, the vast majority of the "new immigrants," are the ones who would build these houses and thus play a fundamental role in the production of the new city and the new neighborhood. Therefore, they participated in producing a new space from which they would later be excluded, in a way similar to the former workers from the South. These are the contradictions in and about space: we want to produce a new neighborhood, attractive to former immigrants and potential middle-class buyers from other localities, but on the other hand, we have the fact that those who build this space (the workers) and who make the exchange possible (tenants or buyers) also live in the neighborhood and also want to participate on a social level.

The historical development of the social construction of the conflict was as follows. In the first place, it arose as a very local problem, that is to say, in the Verge de Núria Street block, and was said to be a problem of space and noise, that is, neighbors struggling to live side by side. Then, when the new location was proposed, a conflict between a few residents of a block became a problem for an entire town. It was no longer a real and experienced *convivencia* conflict, but instead became an abstract and imagined problem of future convivencia, a possible degradation or stigma for the neighborhood or the city and a potential negative impact on the value of homes, in addition to a question of equal rights for everyone to be and inhabit the city and to have a place of worship. Largely thanks to some actors' media exposure and timely political management, it ballooned further into a conflict of regional and State importance and a struggle between natives and immigrants for "cultural *convivencia*." As a result of this balance of the social construction of the problem and its origins, the conflict articulated other conflicts and interests not directly linked to the mosque. The interpretations and discourses of the different social actors appeared to create and transform the conflict strategically, but these explanations do not explain away the conflict given its broader global context and historical setting.

In context, the conflict was characterized by a growth in the number of immigrants to the neighborhood and the city, due to their condition as construction and service workers, and in the Spanish State in general, indicating that the already existing diversity (ethnic, religious and linguistic) was multiplying. It was also characterized by urban transformation. It was a moment of economic change; as the then president of the Spanish government, José María Aznar said, "Spain was doing very well," and many working Spaniards began to have higher consumption levels, supported and promoted by the Spanish bank through mortgages and easy loans. They bought houses and mortgaged and thus internalized the mercantile logic of capitalism. For a minority, the social ascent was very real; for the great majority, it was a mirage, a sweet dream from which they have been rudely awakened. The fundamental changes on the territory were drastic: old neighborhoods and buildings were razed in an enormous process of destruction and reconstruction, the consequences of which were an ever more precarious social and economic state and, therefore, a search for stability and tranquillity. The figure or social category that embodied these changes was, as it usually is, the alien, the stranger, the immigrant: it was at this time that the racial and cultural device of *el moro* was revived (Martín Corrales 2002; Mateo Dieste 1997; Santamaría 2002).

At the city level, these transformations changed, among other things, the structure of the Maresme neighborhood. Not all the inhabitants would enjoy the fruits and privileges of the new situation; rather, they would remain outside of them, even bearing the weight of the stigma. The stigma may have come from living in what some considered the "ghetto" of the city, or because of a fear that their neighborhood would become such a thing without them being able to avoid it or flee it in time. However, it was undoubtedly a very different struggle from those that had been experienced during the final years of the Franco regime and its immediate aftermath (Castells 1973). Instead, this was reactive and vindictive and justifying the exclusion and discrimination of a part of the resident population of the neighborhood and, with it, the general public.

It is plausible that, in the eyes of some inhabitants, their neighborhood was a never-to-be-enjoyed area since it had always been a poorly maintained area with few community facilities. For them, the mosque would confirm this hypothesis and continue the historical trend. Despite the building of the mosque coming with urban improvements, some improvements of which were already paid for was forgotten. Thus, even though the Maresme neighborhood had always been known as a "socialist fiefdom," at the end of the 1990s and the beginning of the new century, many of the residents were adopting and increasingly coinciding with the anti-immigrant discourse from parties such as Plataforma per Catalunya, Partido Popular, and Convergència i Unió.

Although the former immigrants and workers from the Spanish State were part of this movement against construction, although it should be remembered that there were also many who either did not participate or were in favor of the development, the other inhabitants of the residential areas neighboring areas played an important role as well. However, their main concern was not that the neighborhood would become a ghetto or anything like the arguments mentioned above. They had two clear concerns: 1) the tranquillity they had sought in the residential area (the environment they had acquired), and 2) the prices of their homes. The first concern was the congregation of people that the mosque would entail: it would supposedly cause a great deal of noise and hubbub. However, it was the fear of plummeting house prices that became one of the strongest arguments of the most directly exposed residents and other opponents. In fact, the idea was spreading that the mosque's location would mean a loss in the values of the adjacent houses. To avoid the imposition of the mosque and to confirm the more acceptable socio-economic process underway, the former workers of the Spanish State joined with the newcomers from other municipalities in an attempt to expel the undesirables symbolized by the prevention of the new mosque, a symbol par excellence of the presence and possible roots of African immigrants (both those from North and East Africa). The arguments and reasons were different, as I have tried to show. However, finally, the ones that were most widely disseminated, because they underpinned all others, were based on cultural and racial differences that the mosque would only reinforce and that would finally mean a "difficult *convivencia*," arguments that were being naturalized and institutionalized in that historical moment (see for example Azurmendi 2001).

NOTES

1. Euclid was a Greek mathematician from the third century BCE.

2. I have not considered it to be analytically useful to include the subject of gentrification here even though there are processes at work that are quite similar to gentrification (such as, for example, the arrival of people from the middle classes of Barcelona to the old town). This is because it is a controversial concept, and because what could be called gentrifiers are outside the scope of the research of the object of study.

3. I make this distinction of in and on to underline the materiality and ideology of the social construction and production of space.

4. In 1984 the Premià de Mar PGO file was approved, even though it was temporary due to some errors. That is why some plans were already published. Meanwhile, the governing coalition of the City Council had changed from PSC to CIU-ERC.

5. In fact, point b) remains ambiguous enough to mask this desire when it says, "Absorption of growth interpreted restrictively, that is, stopping immigration movements" (PGO-91, 1050), in the points that follow it is done even more evident.

6. These buildings are the most expensive planned. They are two-story homes and in 2010 they were selling for a price between 250,000 and 300,000 euros.

7. In fact, among the informants consulted there is an almost unanimous understanding that the Maresme neighborhood (along with Barri Cotet) had historically been "socialist fiefdoms."

8. David works as a secondary school teacher in a high school in Mataró. Although he had previously been a member of ICV-EUiA and participated in the Coordinator of Premià per la Covivencia, at the time of the fieldwork he was linked to other political movements, such as the Esquerra Anticapitalista Global Revolt and more recently Crida Premianenca.

9. A process that he analyzed in much more depth in Salt (see Lundsteen 2015; Lundsteen 2022).

10. See, for example, Aramburu (2002) and Martínez Veiga (1999), for the cases of Raval and l'Erm respectively.

11. Although there were hardly any remaining in Premià de Mar, there were still in the adjacent towns (Premià de Dalt, Vilassar de Mar i Vilassar de Dalt, and El Masnou) as well as, above all, the regional level.

12. In fact, if we consider the multiple actions in Casc Antic, among others the Special Plan for the protection of architectural heritage and the PE for the modernization of the public space to the historic core, and the current state of the neighborhood, there can be no doubt that there has been a gentrification process.

13. Enric (a graduate in anthropology and economics) worked in an urban planning department in a town next to Premià. At the time of the fieldwork he had been living in Premià de Mar for a short period, where he had arrived from Barcelona. He had also participated in the Coordinadora de Premià por la Covivencia.

14. The vast majority, as I have defended previously, were from Barcelona or working in Barcelona, even though among these there are also immigrants from Western European countries, an increasingly numerous group in Premià de Mar. Take, for example, the statistical report (2007) of the Maresme County Council.

Chapter 4

Cultural Conflicts?

In this chapter we will be following the subsequent ideas of Agamben (2010, 10): "Any research in the human sciences (. . .) should imply archaeological caution, that is, going back in the path itself to the point where something has remained obscure and not themed." Despite an apparent collective selective amnesia, the truth is that *convivencia* conflicts do not arise with extra-community immigration. For this reason, this chapter first proposes outlining an archeology of the discursive interpretations and practices around paradigmatic social conflicts such as those of Ca n'Anglada, El Ejido and Premià de Mar. For this, I have found it helpful to apply the method of archeology of knowledge, as conceived by Michel Foucault (1969). The archaeological method is highly effective for analyzing how some discourses have constituted the migratory phenomenon and how they have facilitated and justified certain social practices. This method aims to clarify the history of some practices by highlighting and connecting previously marginalized or obscured elements (Prado 2000, 24–30). Then, I will reflect on the possible social effects of these policies and ask how diversity and cultural differences are managed in the twenty-first century.

AN ARCHEOLOGY OF "CULTURAL CONFLICTS"

The conflicts surrounding the migratory phenomenon in Catalonia are not new. As I have already pointed out in the first chapter, and as Pere López (1986) recounts in the case of Barcelona, the immigrants from the south of Spain and from within Catalonia itself who arrived in different parts of the Catalan territory in the 1950–1970s, were not well-received; stories of conflict abound. Moreover, these events were often also explained in the context of cultural conflict.

If we jump forward in time to the 1970s, with the arrival of the first immigrants from sub-Saharan Africa, we see how conflicts also arose. On that occasion, however, the conflicts took on a racial element: there was talk of racist attacks, such as when, in Premià, immigrants were attacked in a nightclub. Later, around 1980, another conflict occurred in the Maresme neighborhood, particularly on Carrer de Verge de Núria Street, where the "grey blocks" are located. Conflicts arose around some illicit activities, such as the sale of drugs (what today would be called citizen security), problems that, according to the columnists of the time, were generated by sub-Saharan immigrants. Some residents felt the town council and the police were ignoring their concerns about drug dealing. Together with the support of a local association of Gambians, they took matters into their own hands by monitoring who entered and left the blocks.

Although according to the data,[1] this was the first conflict in the neighborhood about the sale of drugs, there are reasons to doubt that. Furthermore, this type of conflict keeps recurring, as in the year 2000, the issue of drug dealing reappeared, as recounted in chapter 1. This time, however, the culprits of the evil that plagues the neighborhood were of Maghrebi origin: "[A] neighbor (. . .) whose son had suffered a knife attack allegedly at the hands of a Maghreb, called a demonstration to deal with the violent immigrant groups, but also about why they [immigrants] have financial aid when we don't" (Carles 2000).

Without a doubt, this is the substrate of the racist manifestation that we saw in the first chapter. If we examine the arguments of the neighbors we observe an interesting change, since they are at pains not to be perceived as racist:

> Although they did not want to be described as racist, the neighbors argued that living with certain groups of immigrants is difficult and that what happened on Friday "could be repeated and even get worse." The inhabitants of the Verge de Núria Street, a degraded area, accusing them of causing public insecurity and complain, "they occupy the squares and parks, and we cannot take our children there." (Carles 2000)

I wonder whether other types of arguments are gaining importance at this time. Or, perhaps it is no longer so effective, or rather appropriate, to talk about race, but it is much more pertinent and appropriate to talk about *convivencia* and cultural problems. To answer these questions, it is essential to emphasize the historical moment in which the events took place. Two similar and key conflicts for understanding this narrative change preceded it: the conflicts in Ca n'Anglada (Terrassa) and El Ejido. Consequently, in what follows, we will analyze these conflicts with particular attention to the discursive practices that they aroused.

Ca n'Anglada, El Ejido, and Premià de Mar

The number of such conflicts rose sharply at the beginning of the twenty-first century, of which the events of Ca n'Anglada, El Ejido, and finally Premià de Mar were only the beginning. There are elements that bring these apparently isolated events together; the most important is the way they are seen and interpreted. We can observe the appearance of a new rhetoric around social conflicts, and the cases of Ca n'Anglada, El Ejido and Premià de Mar are critical for detecting the discursive change and the implication of this rhetoric in the management by the state.

Among the three, the first major conflict between what have been called "autochthonous and immigrants" in Spain and was picked up by the media occurred in the Ca n'Anglada neighborhood of Terrassa in 1999. Ca n'Anglada is a typical working-class neighborhood in Catalonia. About 20,000 inhabitants reside in the neighborhood, most of whom are from other parts of Spain and often of advanced age. Along with these lives a small proportion of extra-community immigrants, mainly from Africa and especially of Moroccan nationality. The conflicts appear not to have been thoroughly investigated, and the unfolding of events was not precise until recently. Even so, based on a review of 41 articles from the period related to Ca n'Anglada, together with the analysis by Moreras (2004) and Espada and Marimon (2003), I have been able to gather more information, and these form the basis of the following description.

On the evening of July 11, 1999, two neighborhood residents fought while they were at a local party, events that subsequently led to a pitched battle between groups of "indigenous" and "Moroccan" youth. In reality, according to the journalist's account, a real pogrom seemed to have taken place, with "natives" chasing Moroccans, smashing and destroying windows of a bar owned by a Moroccan, a butcher's shop and a place that served as a Muslim place of worship, and therefore a place where Moroccan immigrants (and other Muslims) congregated (Rodríguez 1999a). In the following days, there were similar events, with the police trying to protect Moroccans, until Wednesday the fourteenth, when a demonstration of a clearly racist nature was organized to protest against the presence of Moroccans in the neighborhood; around 1,300 people participated. According to the accounts, there were several "skinheads" in the crowd. One young Moroccan boy was seriously injured with bruises and knocked unconscious by attacks with sticks and motorcycle helmets (Rodríguez 1999b), and a second boy was stabbed (Rodríguez 1999c).

Two days later, a demonstration against racism was held, and three arrests were made in other neighborhoods of Terrassa, two of which were related to the stabbing, and the other on suspicion of incitement to racial violence (the defendant had appeared on television waving knives and inciting their comrades to "go kill Moors"), as well as two thirteen-year-old boys, who had attacked a "ten-year-old black boy" (Rodríguez 1999d). In the following days, things calmed down as more arrests (a total of 11) were made, many of which were related to riots and public order offenses (Rodríguez 1999e).

Finally, on July 27, another demonstration against racism was held, this time led by the mayor, under the slogan "The city of all people," which about 2,200 attended (de Orovio and Rodríguez 1999). A few days later, the Generalitat de Catalunya signed a declaration condemning the racist attacks and supported the demonstrations, urging "the administrations to apply policies that prevent the formation of ghettos and calls on the public to collaborate actively, with respect and tolerance, in the social integration of all those who live in Catalonia" (Editorial Office, *La Vanguardia* 1999).

Half a year later, Terrassa City Council, which had Ca n'Anglada in its purview, proposed several urban renewal projects with the primary objective of "undoing the stigma of the marginalized neighborhood," and thus stimulating investment by the construction sector in new buildings in the area, which, in turn, would tackle the problem of urban degradation (Rodríguez 2000). Or so they hoped.

Not surprisingly, since then, there have been continuous references to Ca n'Anglada. In fact, it is often referred to as the first conflict between natives and immigrants—and this is precisely why it seems of utmost importance. In my opinion, it cannot be argued that it is the first conflict of this type; rather, it was the first time that the media reported a conflict of this type and that it was classified as a conflict between natives and immigrants. Such conflicts would later come to be called *cultural conflicts* or *problems of intercultural convivencia*. By way of exposition, I quote here the words of one of the city councilors: "'We are aware that there are different groups' and that this can create conflicts of *convivencia*" (Rodríguez 1999a).[2] By emphasizing the cultural fact as something that explains away conflict—a conflict that instead has to do with a complex mixture of structural racism, urban degradation and segregation in the real estate market—it ends up linking migration and diversity, presented as a new phenomenon, with conflicts in a cause and effect relationship.

Because of the febrile situation in Terrassa, we also see another trend. At one point, some of the immigrants expressed their desire to demonstrate peacefully, but the town council and the police convinced them not to do so (Rodríguez 1999e). The attacks were directed at symbols of the integration of new migrants, such as Islamic butcher shops and places of worship. Instead of defending the integration of these elements, the racist motivations were not openly confronted and only condemned at the rhetorical level.

This tendency of public administrations to either fear conflict or address it only by paying it lip service, which in my opinion has been the primary mode of operation in dealing with these conflictive situations, is highly problematic, even counterproductive. Moreover, the stance implicitly accepts both the racism of the "autochthonous" populations and their alleged exclusivity in space and over citizenship. In the words of one of the residents of Moroccan nationality, living in Terrassa for over a decade: "It was a kids' fight that someone has manipulated, a cultural and racist conflict has been organized," he argues. "The neighbors are being manipulated, because the people of the neighborhood are demonstrating next to the skins, who are as much our enemies as theirs; they are the scum of society" (de Orovio 1999).

Above all, it is an interesting case because it brings together a large proportion of the elements of the following types of cultural or *convivencia* conflicts: 1) subjective insecurity set in contrast to the lack of official recognition of an objective change, 2) the informal economy of low-level crime, 3) rumors regarding the provision of social benefits only for migrants, 4) the fact that the main parties involved were "Moroccans" and "old migrants," and 5) the context of a working-class neighborhood with the previous history of community ties, that is, a history of the struggle against social degradation and marginalization, first during the Franco regime and, later, with the social consequences of the crisis during the Transition.

Be that as it may, the cultural discourse had not yet been fully institutionalized. I think there are reasons to maintain that it has functioned as a reference and a kind of observatory for future political interventions on immigration and *convivencia*.

In addition to being very famous, the second case of great importance took place in El Ejido, a small town located in Almería, in the southeast of Andalusia.[3] In February 2000, and supposedly in reaction to some murders allegedly committed by a Moroccan, there were several days when tensions in the community ran very high. Residents of Spanish nationality, including many farmers, carried out demonstrations "against the foreign presence," often workers at the farms. There were reports of physical attacks on Moroccan immigrants, property damage, for example, import stores, and a mosque destroyed in an arson attack.

Although at first glance it is one more example of conflicts between natives and immigrants, the interpretation of events is worth exploring as, in this case, the facts help us to reflect on the interpretations made by academic and institutional bodies. Thus, we see how many social researchers intervened in the debate that arose at that time, particularly the anthropologists Ubaldo Martínez Veiga and Emma Martin, who had done fieldwork in the area. However, the one who played a particularly relevant role was Mikel Azurmendi. In fact, this Basque anthropologist established himself as an "expert" during and after the events in El Ejido and came to occupy a fundamental role in establishing a new discursive practice in matters of social conflicts. In 2000, the Popular Party (PP), then in government, created the Forum for the Integration of Immigrants and appointed Azurmendi as president (Narotzky 2005, 46–48).

Without a doubt, one of the most outstanding contributions of Azurmendi was his contribution in institutionalizing a particular vision of the migratory phenomenon, especially the people of the Maghreb, propagating an interpretation very much in line with that propagated by PP. Azurmendi maintained that the attacks had to be interpreted as an almost natural defensive reaction against what the Spanish residents perceived as the undemocratic habits of a people who did not want to assimilate to the "democratic culture" existing in Spain. In fact, despite the violence, he did not even think it appropriate to address the specter of racism. Azurmendi was highly incoherent: he criticized multiculturalism for being essentialist, while, curiously, he argued that Moroccan immigrants did not have an appropriate work ethic or democratic culture. Likewise, he argued that people who did not adapt to the "democratic culture," which he so valiantly defended, should not have the right to question any latent or overt racism:

> Racism occurs, par excellence, in a democratic and legal society because in a society without democratic values, tolerance and pluralism, there is neither racism nor anti-racism because both are ideological positions that are constructed from the perspective of legal and political equality between people considered citizens. (. . .) The Muslim's contempt for the European for being impious and unfaithful is, from the outset, mere religious phobia and cultural xenophobia, without racist implications per se. The current European contempt for Muslims can sometimes carry racist overtones, but not necessarily. So, racism is only something condemnable from democratic and egalitarian positions, not from those that defend that there are subjects and categories of people. The Muslim, for example, is only well placed to condemn racism if he defends a secular culture and democratic values. (Azurmendi 2002)

Thus, following Azurmendi's argument, democratic legal rules become a dominant democratic culture which one must assimilate wholesale to be part of a democratic society. The equalization is easy, even simplistic, and its interpretation becomes the law of a kind of democratic fascism. His argument is based on a very particular interpretation of what democracy and integration mean. Apart from simplifying the facts, Azurmendi also supports the anti-democratic political measures of the PP government, such as the modification of the Immigration Law (Organic Law 8/2000), which reduce the same human rights that he supposedly defends: "Henceforth the strenuous institutional effort required at local and municipal levels to convey good and highly personalized information to immigrants about the habits of our culture, as well as a generous offer so that their expectations are met, at least to a minimum" (Azurmendi 2002).

In my opinion, what can be observed in his writings, apart from the justification of anti-democratic political measures, is a tendency and preponderance, when it comes to explaining or giving meaning to the conflict in El Ejido and thus to subsequent social conflicts, to couch his argument in cultural terms. At the same time, it is shown as an example of the stigmatizing discourse on the "nonintegrable Muslim" (Álvarez 2002), which, as we will see later, is still popular today.

In the case of Premià de Mar, the interpretations drawn from the institutional and administrative instances do not differ too much in terms of underlying factors. Although various arguments appeared, most interpretations were based on cultural factors. Moreover, among the neighbors some gave racist explanations while others proposed less simplistic readings. It is vital to point out that the predominant explanation among most of the participants in the conflict is that it arose from problems of (inter)cultural *convivencia* or of a "cultural conflict" type. What differentiates the interpretations is whether the neighbors are tolerant or not towards cultural differences, open or not, racist, or not, which, in my opinion, shows general concern for cultural differences and the potential for problems that may arise from encountering them.

A good example of this is the report written by the Gabinet d'Estudis Socials (GES 2002). According to the report, racism was at the root of the problem, highly influenced by the media and the general atmosphere owing to the September 11 attacks in the United States. They also concluded that three types of rejection arguments appeared during the conflicts: one that rejected the migration in itself, another rejection of Moroccan immigration and, finally, the rejection of the religion.

If we review the interpretations made both in the media and by the citizens, we see how effectively this type of culture-based explanation is the most dominant; this interpretation has been applied to any social conflict related to the migratory phenomenon. For that reason, one should not be surprised that people begin to fear the presence of immigrants, even if they have not had problems before; apparently, their mere presence leads to conflicts. What has given rise to this xenophobic rhetoric around new immigrants and social conflicts?

The Culturalization of Politics

In the decades after the Second World War, the concept of race began to be replaced by ethnicity as an alternative to discourses based on race in the academic sphere, especially in Europe. In this context, the 1970s saw population changes that occurred with immigration from former colonies, which began to draw more attention in the 1980s, "little by little, through a growing plethora of legal, journalistic, educational, social care, corporate, philanthropic, academic practices, and representations, etc. that take as their object the arrival of migrants, their problems and/or their particularities, make them an increasingly visible social presence and even a generator of moral panic" (Santamaría 2002, 104).

Despite the limited presence of migrants in Spain, the new social category of "the extra-community immigrant" emerged (Santamaría 2002). Along with it, at the end of the 1990s, a discursive shift towards culturalism began. In other words, the concept of culture began to dominate instead of that of race or ethnicity when dealing with difference and, in particular, migration. This discourse and its use stood in contrast to those used and propagated by the academic world, especially anthropology, where the concept of ethnicity had been proposed to combat the extensive use of race.

Several social scientists noted the change at the time. In particular, Étienne Balibar's (1991) description of these new discursive practices is interesting. According to him, he was inspired by Colette Guillaumin (1972) and Pierre-André Taguieff (1995) when he speaks of the existence of a new racism in Europe, which he calls *differential racism* (Balibar 1991, 21, 27). Another notable contribution was that of Verena Stolcke (1995). Despite agreeing with many of Balibar's views, she prefers to speak of *cultural fundamentalism*. According to her, this cultural fundamentalism is a new practice of exclusion, different from racism. His argument is based on the idea that racism is defined as a naturalization of the hierarchical classification of human beings on which it is based, while cultural fundamentalism does not defend any hierarchy as such; it is marked by its differentialism.

In the case of Premià de Mar, we can see how we found the idea of loss of identity among the main arguments against the construction of the mosque; Take, for example, the following quote from Dídac:

> Now, we will not show our face and say that we are against Islam and such . . . No! We are not going to go there, because in that situation, because then they are going to put us here, they are going to sell us to the media, like what? No . . . Now, deep down, we all know that we don't want them . . . but we don't want them, be careful, not for racial reasons, but for cultural reasons . . . I don't know what problems you have up there, but for example, in Holland, it is clear they have problems, and not minor ones . . . they are favoring certain parties . . . that I suppose must be more xenophobic and such, I imagine. (Dídac, sixty-two years old and resident in Casc Antic)

Likewise, in the documentary of the autonomous channel TV3 *Una mesquita a Premià*, we find that most of those interviewed resort to the discourse of cultural fundamentalism. For example:

> They are a very closed people, who do not want to integrate; this is what we see living with them daily. That they have become stiffened, as they were integrating a bit, when the imams arrived (. . .) they began (. . .) to put on headscarves, girls who did not wear them before—people who had lived here for many years, who were integrated, put on a headscarf again. (Maria Àngels Riera, resident of the Maresme neighborhood)
>
> That they adapt to our life . . . We do not have to approach them in their lives, but rather vice versa . . . we welcome them, we give them work, we help them . . . now they shan't impose anything on us . . . they have to adapt to the life that we live. (Joan Ros and Daura Martí, residents of the Banyeres neighborhood)

The ideas described above undoubtedly confirm the hypotheses of neo-racism or cultural fundamentalism. Staying with this confirmation would be somewhat selective, and the statement is more nuanced if we look at the documentary a little more in-depth, since we also find more overt racist speech, as the following excerpts from the TV3 documentary:

> I do not want the mosque on my doorstep, not only because they are Muslims . . . and may the gypsies forgive me, but I would not want any gypsies either . . . no, because they are races that do not get along with . . . very difficult. (Mariano López, resident of the Maresme neighborhood)
>
> I do not want the Moors, I do not want them, I do not want a mosque nor a Moor, that is, I am a Moorish racist, as straightforward as that . . . my son gets up at five in the morning and get up at five in the morning, and go out there with all the Moors with their cones on, it pisses him off . . . and I live on the sixth floor, when I open my window, I see them with their asses with great pomp praying, eh, and it pisses me off a lot. (Anonymous)

Only some resort to the new rhetoric, and it seems that arguments and speeches are mixed. For this reason, and following the argument of Mikel Aramburu (2002), the distinction between the two concepts is unclear to us, or at least, we do not see a discontinuity, but rather, we believe it is relevant to place the use of discourse, thus highlighting the importance of asking ourselves who is speaking? About whom? And where? In what context?

In that sense, a study done in New Zealand, by the distinguished social psychologists Margaret Wetherell and Jonathan Potter (1992), investigated how the use of particular language by the "pākehā" (the local term for whites of European descent) against the "Maori" (the first peoples of Aotearoa/New Zealand), constructed the categories of culture, race, and nation in concrete ways. Although they agreed that in New Zealand, there was a "discursive change," as in Europe, at the same time, they argued that this change had not been completed; the new discursive strategies that have appeared complement each other and overlap existing ones. Therefore, they concluded that racialist discourses did not disappear; on the contrary, a diversity of discursive practices co-exist, containing both culturalist and racial discourses.

Therefore, instead of entering into a sterile academic debate, here I have preferred to use the concept of "cultural differentiation," a concept that Enrique Santamaría (2002, 166–167) developed to address the following paradox: the arguments of cultural fundamentalism and the standard versions of interculturalism or multiculturalism are very much alike (in the version represented by Kymlicka 1995): these are two lines of rhetoric that are undoubtedly different and opposed but that, paradoxically, would come to participate in what we can call a "cultural differentiation" that reduces social relations specific to their cultural dimensions.

Moreover, if we return to Étienne Balibar, we see that he argues that the new discourse carries two crucial political consequences: destabilization of the defenses of traditional anti-racism, in that its argumentation is used against it, and the new discourse can explain or even legitimizing racism. Said in a more detailed way:

1. The new discourse contradicts the arguments of biological racism: it confirms that there are no human races, nor can aptitudes, defects, or behavior be explained through blood or genes; they are the resulting culture. These arguments had been provided by anthropologists and were used against racist arguments and policies. As Balibar argues, we see that "culture" can also naturalize "human behavior" and social affinities: "and it can, in particular, function as a way to classify individuals and groups a priori within a genealogy, within a determination that it is immutable and intangible in origin" (Balibar 1991, 22).
2. The mixing of cultures, or the idea of a melting pot, is seen as the death of "cultural diversity." If it is accepted that the maintenance of cultural distinctiveness is the default state, then when two or more cultures determined to maintain the status quo are thrust together, suspicion and conflict are almost to be expected. These knee-jerk reactions are represented as natural, almost inevitable, yet they are also dangerous and must be avoided. This mindset leads to a political consequence in the need to prevent an outbreak of racist rhetoric or attack.[4] Santamaría writes, "In the practices and representations about 'non-communitarian immigration' the relationship between the presence and characteristics of the migrant collectives with the feelings of concern, fear or alarm that their presence would provoke and the spread of national-populist and/

or neo-racist formations and rhetoric" (2002, 164). This last aspect of
neo-racism that Balibar describes is also the most important because we
find it in the language of public administration.

We face an apparent paradox: the great variety of extant discursive practices are articulated in the same category. The studies undertaken in assessing
the new discursive practices come to meet on one point: the proliferation of
practices of exclusion.

While acknowledging the discourses, one must remember that the new
exclusive practices serve ideological functions since they mask or naturalize
several social issues, including inequalities. This is made evident in terms
such as "cultural diversity" and "cultural difference."[5] The increased usage of
these terms suggests that the media, public administrations, and other entities
are placing high currency on their "cultural impact." This is also evident in
the growing number of foundations and corporate social responsibility programs directly addressing what they perceive as cultural concerns.

In the case of Premià de Mar, the trend is manifested in the interpretations
of the conflict at hand, to the extent that one could speak of a culturalization
of politics. Despite the complexity inherent in all cultural conflicts, which
should be studied in their social, historical and geographical contexts, an
analysis of the reports, articles in the press, opinions of people on the street
indicates that they are based on culture as the determining factor when
explaining the "nature" of these conflicts, that is, they find the ultimate explanation in culture.

One might find an explanation in what Mahmood Mamdani (2004) called
"culture talk," which has since become "common sense" and what Gramsci
would label as hegemonic. It is a way of speaking that makes it possible to
talk only about culture rather than experience it. This may explain why many
of the interpretations from both ends of the spectrum in Premià and other
social conflicts since the end of the 1990s are based on similar assumptions,
namely: the primacy of cultural factors. At the same time, there is an institutionalization of cultural differentiation.

In a very stimulating essay, Manuel Delgado (2006, 1–23), drawing
inspiration from Taguieff (1995), explains how the authorities have adopted
tolerant anti-racism. What Delgado calls "official anti-racism" recognizes the
presence of racism but ascribes it to a racist minority: "There is racism, we
know it. But there is racism not because there is injustice, exploitation, or
poverty . . . there is racism because there are racists" (Delgado 2006, 7). The
institutionalization of this discourse allows talking about racism as something
external, as if it did not affect administrations: This is what the false official
anti-racism has become: a set of theoretical lines that, as Taguieff points out
when speaking of commemorative anti-racism, allows today's well-wishers

to, without real risk or commitment, dedicate themselves to dispensing moral lessons (Delgado 2006, 7).

Furthermore, as we have seen in the three paradigmatic cases, much effort and verbiage are put into preventing these feelings of hatred and fear of the stranger from flourishing, despite being believed to be inevitable. As Aramburu (2002, 264) says: "After the events of Ca n'Anglada in Terrassa and El Ejido, the media tell us almost daily of outbreaks, which everywhere seem to put the *convivencia* between immigrants and natives at risk, establishing an obsessive and alarming climate."

It should be noted that it is through these particular conflicts and moments of tension, what Julio Zino Torrazza calls "social alarm" is built (2006, 33–34). As Agamben (1995) would say, it is the extraordinary that generates the management conditions of the ordinary; it is the logic of the state of exception.

From an observable phenomenon, in this case immigration, and a concomitant discursive paradigm shift, substantial knowledge and discursive practices are produced from which concrete social policies are created. At the same time, an object is marked, the extra-community immigrant, who only becomes visible and "real" at the social level through policies, interventions and discourse.

Today, cultural differentiation is a hegemonic discourse; it has many varieties, and in its popular conception, it is very similar to racial discourse. So strong is its pull that it has also, somewhat worryingly, become hegemonic in the field of social intervention (in municipal and regional administrations, including NGOs),[6] the media and a large part of the academia. The cases that we have seen were in a certain sense representative because the experiences obtained would acquire great importance for future political interventions. As David says:

> [The conflict] transcended the neighborhood, [and] in the end it became a topic that for a month was a subject of constant news on television and such. I know, and in a way, I think that Premià, along with a couple of other towns Terrassa, it seems to me (. . .) became some sort of laboratories for this phenomenon, and in some cases, in the case of Premià, they have exported the solution. (David, forty-eight years old and resident in the Casc Antic neighborhood)

Let us see more clearly what effects this culturalization of politics has on the local management of social conflicts.

CONFLICT MANAGEMENT

This section will deal with the management of cultural diversity and, more specifically, the political practices around the migration phenomenon. We will see the specific social policies and how they reproduce the same problems they were supposed to solve. The discursive change detected in the previous section directly affects political practices and the measures taken by municipalities (Reeves et al. 2009; Moreras 2009), in addition to the interpretations made by the media and, in part, by the inhabitants. I am not referring to a simple ideological function. I intend to demonstrate how from a particular situation, a series of discursive and practical, social actions unfolds that end up dispossessing some people of fundamental civil and socioeconomic rights to promote a discourse that justifies this same action and ends up reproducing the cultural difference and the groupings around it.

In the mid-1980s, two events, Spain's entering the European Union and the "new" extra-community migration, led to new various social policies being implemented (Zapata 2003; Gil Araujo 2010). The policies, effectively socio-regulatory practices, were aimed at the "new migratory phenomenon" and have, since the early 1990s, emphasized three aspects of community management: the control of flows of migration, the prevention of the causes for immigration, and the integration of immigrants and their families who are deemed to be "legally" installed (Santamaría 2002, 132).

Since then, immigration has been presented as a problem of citizen security and culture; however, it was not until the beginning of the twenty-first century that the idea strongly emerges that immigration is a problem of other cultural beings, who must be integrated emphasizing the (inter)cultural aspects (Gil Araujo 2010). Specifically, from the emblematic social conflicts described in the introduction, a change can be detected in how social issues around immigration are handled. From the viewpoint of these representative cases, the discourse of "cultural differentiation" around various social conflicts begins to be institutionalized, and then social and integration policies are proposed for their solution.

Thus, there is a growing institutionalization of discourses and rhetoric around this "new" migratory phenomenon, which coincide in underlining cultural diversity in the face of any other social condition. There is a growing concern for cultural aspects, which is manifested, as earlier noted, through such buzz words as "cultural diversity" and "cultural difference," to name just two.

The strategic plans drawn up by the Spanish State (MTI 2007, 2011) and the national pact of the Generalitat de Catalunya (GC 2008, 2009, 2012, 2014) must be considered. These essential documents outline a model to be followed at the administrative level across the communities in which the problem of "residential concentration" is of particular importance, as it is argued that an imbalance could give rise to so-called ghettoization and hostilities between Spanish and foreign neighbors. Although the crisis is mentioned on several occasions as a factor to consider, behind the idea of "ghettoization" is the assumption that the problems in impoverished urban areas have to do with the concentration of "cultural minorities" and people with special needs. According to this diagnosis, "the intercultural *convivencia* of citizens in the neighborhoods" is promoted (MTI 2011, 116) to overcome potential hostile situations.

In the Catalan case, this translates into a commitment to the continuity of the program known as Llei de Barris[7] (GC 2009, 115) and for the maintenance of actions such as allowances to "subsidize rents in households at risk of social exclusion, including immigrants at risk of housing exclusion" (GC 2008, 58). In addition, it aims to promote intercultural *convivencia* in the public space (GC 2008, 66; MTI 2011, 318) and community projects "developing urban cohesion policies, and measures in favor of community projects, neighborhood improvement, civic participation, and association" (GC 2012, 4). This is translated into measures addressing diversity in a circuitous attempt to solve the problems that supposedly arise from it (Gil Araujo 2010; Agrela Romero 2006; Moreras 2009).

From the conflicts that I have set out, we can observe a change in how social issues around immigration are addressed, and the attempts at management. We see how the public administration and the media begin to institutionalize the discourse of cultural differentiation around various social conflicts and then propose policies for their solution. In other words, we see a culturalization of interventions (social policies) around social conflicts. In fact, Moreras (2004, 445) supports this initial hypothesis by stating that, in the context of Catalonia, it was the conflicts in the Ca n'Anglada de Terrassa neighborhood (1999), the conflict in the l'Erm neighborhood of Manlleu (1999) and the conflict of the mosque in Premià de Mar, that proved most decisive for future political actions and adds:

> These three cases may have represented a significant turning point in how local immigration intervention policies are thought, designed, and formulated. The new paradigm that seems to be proposed passes through the field of "diversity management," which starts from a double preventive and regulatory assumption of the circumstances involved in intercultural *convivencia*.

In the case of Ca n'Anglada, we have an interesting example. On the part of the town council and the Generalitat de Catalunya, a commission of experts was constituted to analyze the causes of the conflict, and this commission later proposed solutions:

> Urban programs [aimed] at generating a higher quality of urban space that facilitates the cohesion and integration of its inhabitants and contributing to the *convivencia* of each of the four neighborhoods integrated in the district and in the city. For their part, the Social Programs have been conceived, beyond the specific objectives described above, to generate new opportunities and relationship dynamics that provide the renewed urban environment with a dimension of well-being and social enjoyment. (Martínez Soler and Terrassa City Council 2008)

In 2002, the Terrassa City Council launched a project that sought the comprehensive renovation of the neighborhood, and in 2004 the Generalitat de Catalunya contributed more money through the Llei de Barris to implement pilot projects and social programs, in addition to carrying out development and infrastructure improvements. The apparent logic was to reply on urban planning to create a new, problem-free space, the social life of the neighborhood should be improved and encourage good relations between the inhabitants. That is to say: space is seen as determining. It is not the first time an attempt has been made to solve social problems by resorting to urban planning, nor will it be the last.

In the case of Premià de Mar, we see how the political bodies proposed to create an institutional body for dialogue, the Municipal Council for Convivencia (CMC). This strategy has been attempted several times to solve conflicts of cultural *convivencia*,[8] with Salt (2010) as the latest example (Lundsteen 2015, 2022). The CMC was formally established as part of the conflict resolution exercise and was located in the same buildings as the provisional mosque at Escola Voramar. Following the description of the Consell Comarcall de Maresme (CCM) it was "a panel for dialogue, debate and proposals on issues of *convivencia*, integration and socio-cultural values."

The initial plan was for it to be an organization that would work "for the reconstruction of a civic *convivència* in Premià de Mar among people of different cultures" (Editorial Office, *La Razón* 2002). The CMC would include representatives of all local entities that would like to work for this cause, and thus "the regulation is a starting point to start working for *convivència*, intercultural dialogue and social integration of people" (Ansola 2002c). The body would also "seek, in the long term, a definitive location for the Muslim oratory" (J. V. 2002).

In 2003, the first meeting was held, and 30 entities participated, among which were the neighborhood associations of Banyeres, now Banyeres-Solimar-Nou Premià, and of Tarter-Maresme, in addition to AIAT and new immigrant

associations from Prize. The CMC made several proposals in its initial meetings, including attending the 2004 Universal Forum of Cultures: "The idea
is to propose an urban study linked to the *convivencia* between different cultures. The intention is to offer Premià de Mar as a pilot experience on urban
planning for convivencia and take advantage of all the ideas and resources
that may arise" (Maresme County Council Press Service 2003). Another of
the proposals was to identify the problems of convivencia (in a generic way
the councilor of social services assured) that the municipality can manage.
Thus, they dealt with matters related to rent, work, knowledge of the language, and the culture and customs of each group. Finally, after some time
and a change in membership of the council, they began to discuss making
some amendments to the constitution of the CMC:

> The government, made up of CiU and ERC, is studying the approach that this
> panel should have for the future. Most of the members of the government team
> believe that the Consell de la Convivència should be framed entirely in the
> cultural sphere. In this way, the issue of immigration would be avoided from
> a social services perspective and a conflictual point of view. The councilor for
> social services and education, Mercè Gisbert (ERC), assures that the council's
> work will continue but that now it is necessary to rethink how it works. Gisbert
> favors this body, becoming dependent on the Department of Culture to deal with
> immigration issues naturally. "We have to talk about immigration from a cultural
> perspective to normalize the treatments," added the councilor. (Ansola 2003)[9]

Another initiative was, as I mentioned at the end of chapter 1, the Pacte per
la Nova Ciutadania (2002). When the AIAT signed the agreement on using
the Escola Voramar buildings, it also had to sign and give assent to this new
citizenship pact. Perhaps it would have been more correct to call it a social
contract, since it states, for example, that "is a commitment of its signatories
to work for a city model based on social cohesion, *convivencia*, citizenship
and equal opportunities, and that responds to the new needs and changes that
immigration represents."

The three strategic lines that define the pact are the following:

> 1) the integration of newcomers within the framework of respect for democratic
> principles and values, guaranteeing the rights and duties of citizenship, 2) the
> normalization of the provision of services, equal opportunities, and quality of
> life of all citizens, 3) the promotion of social and cultural change, cohesion and
> *convivencia*, from the consensus and social and political consensus in the city.
> (Premià de Mar City Council 2002)

Among the action programs "aimed at the integration of newcomers, *convivencia*, respect for diversity, and the quality of life of citizens" we find that

many contain the word "intercultural," and one, in particular, draws attention: "Cultural diversity: favoring cultural exchange through the promotion of knowledge of the different cultural manifestations of the city."

Given the history that I have outlined, we have been able to see how a discourse of culture has been politicized, what I have termed a culturalization of politics. I argue that Ca n'Anglada, El Ejido and Premià de Mar were representative examples of new cultural-social relations and new cultural-social conflicts. These same towns would become laboratories for political and regulatory experimentation without seriously considering the potential conflicts in their wake. Beginning with the policies tested in Premià de Mar, similar agreements have been approved and implemented in other Catalan municipalities, including L'Hospitalet de Llobregat, Terrassa, Sabadell, and El Masnou.

These plans shared a basic principle: politically, it was necessary to manage a social complexity perceived as the result of the new migration patterns. We can also observe projects at a more regional level, the objective being to implement social policies, such as in the Maresme Regional Council where a whole body was created, the Servei del Pla Territorial de Ciutadania i Immigració, to coordinate social policies around this supposedly novel situation. Although it is beyond this research to offer a detailed description of this body, I would only like to mention that it is composed of technocrats who write reports on migration and conflicts supposedly linked to it, such as the conflict of the mosque in Premià de Mar. In addition, the body allocates money to projects that align with the objectives of the Regional Plan so that, from this general and normative plan, policies are made, and funding is given to avoid the harmful effects of immigration. I have been able to access some of his studies, of which the most interesting has been the Estudi Prospectiu d'Immigració a la Comarca del Maresme of 2003; a study that dedicates a whole section to the theme of "Culte Religiós Musulmà." One is bound to ask how these discourses and policies at the macro level are related to the social relations between the inhabitants.[10]

The consequences of these social policies of cultural diversity and intercultural *convivencia* can certainly be very diverse; however, the object of the intervention, the social reality assumed at the beginning of its epistemological point of view, becomes a product of the policies. Social subjects and the relationships they establish between them are limited, in this case, to their cultural expression. Here, I draw from Loïc Wacquant (2007), although he does not say it explicitly: when the concept of the ghetto, instead of *banlieues*, appeared in France, a different device was institutionalized. The device, which operated through social interventions, ordered reality differently and created, through this same process, the very object of the interventions: the ghettos.

Following this line of argument, one could deduce that the devices derived from the culturalization of politics foster social relations based on cultural affiliation. The inhabitants internalize these devices through teaching, awareness, and the influence of the media. This process of internalization resembles what Michel Foucault (2006) called governmentality. Indeed, following his ideas, Carol Bacchi postulates that policies do not constitute an optimal government response to an existing "problem," but rather that policies themselves produce "problems" through the problematization of certain groups or events. Her approach is based on the premise that contemporary society is governed by the repeated creation of accepted political truths (truth policies) by those in power. Policies are here discursive practices that construct the "problems"; they articulate them in line with an ideological agenda and propose specific "political solutions" (Bacchi 2010). In this way, political discourse is defined as "forms of social knowledge that make it difficult to speak outside the terms of reference that they establish to think about people and social relations" (Bacchi 2009, 35).

Thus the discourses of cultural differentiation crystallize through social policies that later give rise to a series of determined social practices, in such a way that (cultural) devices adopt materiality and groupings become cultural collectives: social facts, almost natural, to which each of us is affiliated whether we want to be or not. Moreover, the social relations between those would be limited by "culturalized social practices." In other words, these devices would complicate other types of reading, such as from political economy, and therefore the subjects become culturalized subjects. In this way, one learns to explain and understand reality according to these cultural discourses. In the words of Manuel Delgado (1998, 28): "If we recognize that most conflicts between communities are not due to their identity traits, as it might seem due to the illusion of the autonomy of cultural facts, but to conflicting interests, cultural diversity appears as a much more relative source of conflicts than what we often think."

Although the conflicts discussed here have a very varied discursive materiality (remember that the arguments and discursive practices were by no means homogeneous), they were interpreted in a very concrete way: through a cultural paradigm. This paradigm has had an essential influence on actions directed towards "social matters" in the city. It supported and even gave rise to interventions now in the cultural sphere or, rather, in the culturalized social sphere. In other words, it promoted social policies directed towards cultural diversity or the promotion of intercultural *convivencia*, and so on. Now, we have just seen how these policies become truths, in ways of seeing the world: by creating devices. I would like to address two issues that seemed to be addressed by this more structural analysis.

When analyzing discursive practices closely, we can discern that, although the available repertoire is the same for all groups of inhabitants, each one follows specific guidelines in practice.

In the first place, I have already noted that there is no substitution of discursive practices. In other words, cultural differentiation is not the only discursive practice we have come across: we have also seen others based on the nineteenth-century ideas of race. We see, for example, how people from the working classes, and the older population, tend to use racial discursive practices. In contrast, the middle-class residents adopt politically correct discourses of cultural differentiation (remember that by this, we also refer to the right-minded versions). I am not just referring to the fact that some use one type of discourse and others another; it also seems to depend on the subject they are talking about.

In some cases, more racial discourses are used, and in other moments they are cultural. Thus, physiognomic aspects are often highlighted when it comes to Senegalese or Gambians. People speak of "Blacks" or "brunettes," and often a paternalistic attitude is maintained, notable through the use of the diminutive. On the contrary, when speaking of Moroccans, cultural terms predominate, and a rhetoric of competitiveness and segregation or assimilation is employed when speaking of their adaptation. Perhaps this difference has something to do with the proximity and similarity of the Moroccans, both in geographical and historical terms and in physical appearance. I suggest that this shows that some language is better suited to some subjects than others. Perhaps even though the Catalans feel the need to differentiate themselves from the Moroccan, it is still inappropriate to speak of a different race, hence the reliance on cultural terms.

> They have a way of living, a way of being totally different from ours . . . with which . . . This is the existing rejection . . . but it is not a racial one . . . because look at myself, I have Arab features, well I don't give a damn, it's clear, it's the same to me absolutely, I don't have any complexes . . . But I mentally, culturally . . . I am the antithesis of those people . . . In Europe, it is something different. (Dídac, sixty-two years old and resident in Casc Antic)

Now, although the central subject of the mosque controversy is the Muslim, it should be noted that in the three cases that have been mentioned, the object of the aggressions and polemics, that is, in the interpretations, is the Muslim Arab often referred to as "el moro."[11] In addition, it is significant that throughout the fieldwork and in the archive, a constant mistake can be seen. "Muslim" is equated with "Moroccan," when in fact, many of the believers are also Senegalese and Gambian, and there are non-Muslim Moroccans. In Enric's words,

There the Muslim concept was mixed with the Moroccan concept, right? . . .
That is, a problem arose, of *convivencia* . . . The starting point was the mosque
construction, but in reality, a religious question was not being raised; it was an
ethnic question. (Enric, thirty-eight years old and resident in Casc Antic)

The big question is undoubtedly whether the rejection reaction has to do
with religion, of what some have called Islamophobia, or instead of one
Arabophobia or anti-Muslim racism.[12] Étienne Balibar (1991, 23–24) makes
the following comment on the subject:

A racism which does not have the pseudo-biological concept of race as its
main driving force has always existed, and it has existed at exactly this
level of secondary theoretical elaborations. Its prototype is anti-Semitism.
Modern anti-Semitism, the form which begins to crystallize in the Europe of
the Enlightenment, if not indeed from the period in which the Spain of the
Reconquista and the Inquisition gave a statist, nationalistic inflexion to theologi-
cal anti-Judaism is already a "culturalist" racism. Admittedly, bodily stigmata
play a great role in its phantasmatics, but they do so more as signs of a deep
psychology, as signs of a spiritual inheritance rather than a biological hered-
ity. These signs are, so to speak, the more revealing for being the less visible
and the Jew is more "ruly" a Jew the more indiscernible he is. His essence is
that of a cultural tradition, a ferment of moral disintegration. Anti-Semitism is
supremely "differentialist" and in many respects the whole of current differentia
list racism may be considered, from the formal point of view, as a generalized
anti-Semitism. This consideration is particularly important for the interpretation of contemporary Arabophobia, especially in France, since it carries with it
an image of Islam as a "conception of the world" which is incompatible with
Europeanness and an enterprise of universal ideological domination, and therefore a systematic confusion of "Arabness" and "Islamicism."

This brings us full circle to the debate on the difference between racism and
culturalism. In addition, as Balibar said, Islamophobia and the image of the
Moor fit very well with the new discourses of cultural differentiation.

Before concluding, I would just like to underline one crucial point. With
this chapter, I do not intend to affirm that there are no social differences of a
cultural nature, but what I have wanted to do is draw attention to how a particular interpretation of this concept is being used politically, and that far from
helping ethnic or cultural minorities, they are captured in their own banalized
and commodified expression. Moreover, under the shield of good intentions,
social policies are created, supposedly to help "the poor immigrants," when
the objectives in many cases show to be the same as always: to satisfy the
need to control some subjects that induce fear in the middle classes because
of their different way of being, in addition to their poor or miserable condition. They are cultural social policies that aim to control immigrants and

educate them to be immigrants and civilized. We leave the question open: why have social policies directed to immigrants emphasizing culture been implemented?

NOTES

1. Remember, these come from an exhaustive review of the existing press clippings in the Gómez-Fontanills Archive (AGF).

2. The first part of this quote is are the words of the councilman, the rest is the journalist.

3. I follow here the interpretations of Martínez Veiga (2001) and Zino Torraza (2006).

4. Regarding the de-dramatizing use of words such as outbreak and xenophobia, Santamaría says: "It is often insistently stated that, in reality, it is not about racism but about classism or xenophobia, as if thereby losing importance, as if the action, when being an aggression against poor foreigners instead of being against individuals or groups of another race, would not have the same seriousness" (Santamaría 2002, 163).

5. Among the contributions made, the conclusions on the political use of culture present in the declaration of the IX Congress of Anthropology of the Federation of Anthropology Associations of the Spanish State 2002 seem particularly correct.

6. An example could be the work of Jordi Pascual and Jonathan Sánchez: "La convivència intercultural a Premià de Mar" (2005). I do not doubt that they had the best intentions, in fact, they begin with a fundamental questioning of social relations, but in my opinion they do not manage to get out of this cultural paradigm at all.

7. *Llei 2/2004 de millora de barris, àrees urbanes i viles*, was the first law in the Spanish State aimed at improving neighborhoods as a unit of action. It was implemented in the first period of the Tripartite government, with the explicit intention of establishing a comprehensive rehabilitation program in those urban areas that required special attention, and forecasted investing 600 million euros until 2011 to improve the living conditions of citizens in those areas.

8. It was not the first example of a council of this type in Catalonia. In 1997, the Municipal Immigration Council was formed in Barcelona. Despite this, it was not directly linked to issues of social cohesion, intercultural *convivencia*, or cultural diversity, rather it was an attempt to promote the political participation of new immigrants.

9. As the councilor explained to me, this mixture did not create a good atmosphere, she says: "It was not an adequate format, it did not lead to anything a month other than to meet groups facing each other and take advantage of the space to throw things away." Joana fifty-five years old and resident in the Casc Antic.

10. Although it is undoubtedly a very important and interesting question, unfortunately, due to the limitations of the work, I have not been able to deal with it in depth or in a satisfactory way, but I have had to limit myself to broad strokes.

11. See Lundsteen (2018) for a historical overview of this concept.

12. I deal with this question in much greater depth in later publications such as Lundsteen and Shaimi (In revision).

Conclusions

While being aware of the somewhat vague and general quality of this statement, I would say that every ethnographic approach has a prime objective: to construct data on the foundation of the existing social universe to better understand the human condition. This primary function of fieldwork leads the anthropologist to become part of the social space in search of informative units and indicators from which to build systematic knowledge of human affairs.

The fundamental objective of this research has been to explore the relationships between migratory movements and processes of social and spatial hierarchy within the framework of capitalist geography. This starting point meant that many areas could have provided essential data. Among all of them, I decided to focus on the reality of the coastal town of Premià de Mar, where the upheavals of contemporary historical and economic processes have created a privileged case in which to set my initial questions.

Premià de Mar meets the essential structural characteristics of a municipality in transformation due to the territorial integration processes typical of existing contemporary capitalism. It has a recent and very significant experience of social conflict around the uses and appropriation of land and space: namely that in 1997, the construction of a mosque was planned in the heart of the Maresme neighborhood. The proposal divided the neighborhood. Why the positioning of neighbor against neighbor? What motives led to the opposition to the creation of a community space? Moreover, beyond the discursive devices in use, what kind of conflict was being staged after the appearance of an ethno-racial confrontation?

This series of questions highlighted the need to identify and recognize the complex network of variables required to understand the process. An investigation was launched to determine the specific context (temporal and spatial) in which the site was located, during which we saw how the neighborhood prepared for a significant transformation in the creation of two residential developments, located on either side of the land where the new mosque was to be built. The composition of the place was: a new city-garden area, set around almost identical semi-detached houses. This space was marketed to the upper-middle classes from the Barcelona exodus. The southern part of the Maresme neighborhood was being transformed, too, designed to be especially attractive to former immigrants from southern Spain by giving it a veneer of upward mobility.

Flanked by the developments and their internalized narratives, along with a simmering Islamophobia, the mosque did not fit in. Indeed many of the opponents to the mosque came from the new homes, so I have proposed that the desire to prevent the mosque from being built was driven by the desire to limit the presence of degrading elements and subjects.

Consequently, although those who subscribe to Islam have rights equal to all other people of faith, these rights are often questioned, relegated, or ignored in practice. Despite the congregation's readiness to proceed with the construction, full permission was never granted—it was given formally, but, in the background, it was communicated to the Muslim community that it would behoove them to relinquish their rights and co-operate in the maintenance of social order and co-existence.

Now, social conflicts in and over space, as we have shown in the case of the mosque, are not perceived as spatial. Instead, they are territorial conflicts, where space appears as a mere habitat in which some social groups fight, leading to different expressions of NIMBYism. The idea of an effect or process of the NIMBY, who fight the "offensive" by crying Not In My Back Yard, explains the phenomenon of opposing buildings or developments are perceived as undesirable or dangerous (in many cases, they are constructions of prisons, rehabilitation centers, nuclear power plants, etc.). I could apply an analysis of the NIMBY effect to the cases studied here. However, I have not found this reading very useful, since on the one hand, it seems to be a very vague concept, and, on the other, because it is one of many modes of this class of arguments, which center on what is politically correct and explicitly resolved to cover up less accepted discourses.

A change in Spanish immigration policy at the beginning of the twenty-first century made it easier to control migratory flows, and from this came the stigmatizing campaign against Moroccan immigration, one of the largest groups of migrants in the country. In this context, exceptional events such as those at Ca n'Anglada, El Ejido, and Premià de Mar conflicts were paradigmatic examples. A new logic emerged with immigration as a problem to be managed; it became a phenomenon that created conflicts. The discourse of cultural differentiation, in addition to refusing to question social and economic inequalities in depth, supported this hypothesis and relegated the issue to cultural conditioning factors.

Urban conflicts have a diverse nature, but despite the deep-seated desire to avoid conflict (Moreras 2004), there are increasing disagreements over space and spatial contradictions, which are usually explained in other terms, such as an incompatibility of lifestyles or difficulties in the coexistence of a plurality of cultures and religions. From these conflicts has developed a cultural device that explains the social space (the relationships between the inhabitants and the neighborhood conflicts) in cultural terms is being institutionalized. This narrative stigmatizes migrants, especially Moroccans, as they are the most prominent minority. From the conflict, a stigma around Moroccans and what is considered Moroccan and, in particular, Islam becomes visible: a process that corresponds to what Pierre Bourdieu called symbolic violence (Bourdieu 2007).

I have argued that this culturalization of politics has normalized talking about cultures and that it has crystallized through the promulgation of social policies that confirm the same cultural differences. The policies are devices of power internalized by the citizens, even though there is relatively little difference between the supposedly different groups: neighbors, workers, and immigrants. Around this common point, there is a link that could be used to promote better *convivencia* (which should not imply no conflicts), a link that would not divide a population that, in the beginning, may well have the same interests in terms of improving their material conditions.

As I have shown, while in earlier decades, social conflicts were often understood and thought of in terms of social class, today, this convergence that previously brought together (that did not unite) the working classes through political or union grouping is not well-articulated. On the contrary, what we see is that a part of the working class joins with a part of the middle class (with less cultural capital), and on the other side, the other part of what would be the working class, or remains alone, or he meets, as is the case here, with another part of the middle class (with more cultural capital). If the unions and left-wing parties are no longer as strong as before, it certainly has to do with this. The challenge is then how to articulate this contradiction in a more coherent way that makes sense for all actors, if possible, and if not, to at least find a way to fight collectively that is not as fragmentary as currently, and yet at the same time does not oppose each other; although there might indeed be differences in terms of privilege and interests. In the end, recalling the general ideas of the Black radical tradition (Robinson 2000; Haider 2018), it is of no interest to the social groups comprehended amongst the working classes that the inhabitants of a neighborhood, a town, a nation, feel or are excluded from the citizenry; it creates fractions that weaken any struggle for social equality and fairness. However, what is more, when *some* are singled out, it potentially singles us all out.

From the analysis of the conflicts in Premià de Mar, we have seen how the culturalization of politics conceals these contradictions in supposed conflicts of intercultural coexistence: that is, it inhibits the readings attentive to the underlying sociospatial contradictions. I have shown that the geography of capitalism produces social inequalities in terms of civil, social, and economic rights, which are presented as contradictions over space, as Henri Lefebvre (1991, 365) affirmed: "Sociopolitical contradictions are realized spatially. The contradictions of space thus make contradictions of social relations operative. In other words, spatial contradictions 'express' conflicts between socio-political interests and forces; it is only in space that such conflicts come effectively into play, and in so doing they become contradictions of space."

The explanations argue either that there is an incompatibility between specific cultures perceived as static and homogeneous or that the immigrant does not want or seek integration into the "host society." I have tried to show that it is a fallacious paradigm, a product of a growing concern to avoid any form of open conflict, and a need to redirect conflicts, when they do appear, towards other non-harmful explanations against the hegemonic political, legal, economic and cultural system. The case shows precisely that the deployment of capitalism in and on space requires legitimizing discourse. In this process of self-legitimation and reproduction of the capitalist system, NGOs, public administrations, and the State in general play a decisive role by implementing and sustaining cultural differentialism.

> In fact, if the different institutional sources have something in common when faced with this type of conflict, they tend to label them as punctual vandalism by intolerant minorities that do not reflect the feelings of the majority. This position, the defense of this point of view that does not directly attack the xenophobic background of these conflicts, is, in the opinion of the anti-racist movement, a breeding ground that does nothing to stop their proliferation. (Pelàez 2002)

Many readings of social conflicts about mosques consider the space a mere container of these conflicts or represent them as "territorial conflicts," where the space is a mere habitat for the domain from which some social groups struggle. On the contrary, what I have tried to argue with this research is that space is a social, dynamic and continuous construction, and specifically under capitalist geography, it tends to have several functions that flow into and away from one another: it is a means of production and reproduction, and a product to be sold and consumed. In the ebb and flow, conflicts occur, and that is why we would have to include this spatial dimension in our analysis when dealing with conflicts of this nature.

In order to offer an alternative reading, this book has lent itself to a Lefebvrian reading of "the production of space" (Lefebvre 1991) that exposes the social and economic processes inherent to the creation of space that, in the case of the mosque conflicts had not been sufficiently analyzed. The interpretations made about some social conflicts between what was labelled as autochthonous and immigrant populations provided the arguments to explain the conflict over the mosque in terms of racial, ethnic or cultural conflict. These social representations eventually became dominant. A mistake was made from the start: too much attention was given to cultural factors as if these could be sui generis, that is, completely independent of social, economic or political factors and processes. Alternatively, and rescuing the ideas presented by Peláez in the previous quote, the idea that racism was present in only an intolerant minority emerged, thus omitting institutional racism and the social and economic structures on which they are based and with which they interact, a "conceptual torsion," as defined by Taguieff (1995).

Where any social conflict seems to take the appearance of a conflict of cultural coexistence or ethnic/racial conflict, either due to tensions over the construction of a place of worship or because of the so-called social insecurity, attention must be drawn to the disguising of systemic prejudices. In the representation of the nature and cause of social conflicts, the media play a fundamental role, as do academics, public institutions, and NGOs. Their (mis)representations participate in the constitution and imagination of what the problems are and what solutions should be employed.

The conclusions and interpretations drawn from the Premià de Mar conflict, mainly those offered by public institutions and NGOs, have given rise to interventions by public administrations that have had a rather inhibitory nature, in the sense of wanting to avoid open conflict by whatever means. The effects of the policies often marginalize the Muslim communities in question, in addition to establishing a legal lacuna, by which I mean the situation of inequality faced by Muslim communities and other religious communities in the Spanish State when it comes to having places of worship when compared with the Catholic Church. There is a vast disproportion between the number of Muslims and their places of worship, many of which are less than suitable. I think it would be correct to classify the silent acceptance of the legal lacuna in the social and religious context of the Spanish State as problematic at the very least.

If the case of Premià de Mar shows us anything, it is the wide range of factors that must be taken into account when analyzing and explaining the conflicts over mosques, and that when treating them, one should not limit the analysis to a cultural or psychological interpretive framework. It is essential to pay attention to the geographical-historical context that they take place on and in. Moreover, the matter no longer requires objectivity—which, although we can pursue it, we will never achieve it at all—but a reflection on the role we play in interpreting the facts and conflicts around the places of worship.

The case of Premià de Mar points to a standard error in the studies of conflicts over mosques and, to a certain extent, migratory studies in general: the interpretations focus only on cultural factors, as if one could speak of culture per se, entirely unrelated for socio-economic and political factors and processes. On the other hand, racism is perceived as a trait of an intolerant minority (reflecting what Miles and Brown [2003] describe as "racism as a moral issue"), without taking into account institutional and structural racism and its interrelationship with socio-economic structures.

Since the Premià de Mar conflicts, a line of preventive action has been instituted in Catalonia, in which both the communities themselves and the municipal administrations have increasingly chosen to locate mosques in industrial areas. In my opinion, these trends should be viewed with suspicion. Large tracts of land can often be found where it would be possible to construct a building as a place of worship, that is, a mosque instead of an oratory in a garage, but, beyond that, the advantages are few. In this way, instead of incorporating minority religious practices into the recognized religious pluralism of the Spanish State and the urban space of the neighborhoods, and facing any conflict that this could bring, they have chosen to hide them. These policies of concealment and silencing of Muslim religious practices and symbols end up reproducing the stigmatized and suspicious image that weighs on Muslims today in the Spanish and broader European contexts (Bravo López 2012; López Bargados 2009; Prado 2009), in addition to reinforcing the more conservative and segregationist currents in general.

This complex social phenomenon has been labelled Islamophobia. However, although there are several ways of conceptualizing this, the hegemonic conceptions of Islamophobia tend to relegate the problem to the psychological realm as something pathological and fundamentally individual, thus ignoring the social and structural characteristics of the phenomenon. These interpretations of Islamophobia as an ideology (Miles and Brown 2003) bear much resemblance to what elsewhere has been described as "cultural talk" (Mamdani 2004), in which complex social phenomena are reduced to mere cultural or religious questions. In that sense, it is relevant to remember that Islamophobia arose mainly in the Global North and that it is closely related to migration owing to the necessity for the poor in the Global South to move towards the Global North. Further exacerbation comes from an intensification of accumulation by extra-European dispossession through imperialist wars and practices in the Middle East, all of which is playing out in a period of local-global restructuring of economies and power relations often (though not completely satisfactorily) referred to as "neoliberalism."

What seems clear is that Islamophobia in its most abstract version is closely related to the changing geopolitical landscape of the "triumph of neoliberalism," as other authors have recognized (Lean 2012; Kumar 2012).

Indeed, it might be helpful to apprehend it as a structural explanation, an ideology of neoliberalism, a political-economic project in itself. However, while these kinds of narratives are useful for "big capital" interests, they are also very convenient for the "native" working class, often uncomfortable with the new neighbors. This vision promotes a vision of society in which they have more rights than newcomers, especially when postwar social achievements are threatened in terms of working conditions and wages, and their children's future is thought to be at risk. However, the case of Premià de Mar reminds us of the dangers of reducing the racist expressions present in many neighborhoods in the West to a simple myopic reproduction of these abstract discourses. Contemporary anti-racist struggles often focus on anti-Muslim racism as a struggle for recognition, often disconnected from the general struggle against the material forces that sustain and interact with it, a point that has recently been pointed out by several other authors (Müller-Uri and Opratko 2016; Haider 2018).

This book shows how conflicts presented as ethnic or (inter)cultural conflicts can operate with much more complex social phenomena. In this case, the underlying factors that gave rise to the theatrical conflicts exposed in the media also addressed specific economic and political interests, a product of increasing commercialization of space in the neighborhood where the mosque was supposed to be built. Drawing attention to this issue should encourage further debate on the importance of space in the analysis of mosque conflicts and the importance of academic and media representations in the production of the problem: referring to mosque conflicts as yet another expression Islamophobia is too abstract and could fundamentally disconnect them from other related social factors, be they political, economic or both. We must substantiate and broaden the analysis to recognize and understand the phenomenon's complexity.

At the same time, however, another consideration must be made, as well. As I reviewed the original manuscript from 2015, I found myself finishing a report on Islamophobia in Catalonia. The first thing that surprised me was how the conflicts around mosques and oratories had not ceased since this first paradigmatic conflict, already more than twenty years ago. Moreover, it is surprising that the forms of opposition today are so similar to those found in Premià de Mar during those initial years of the new millennium. How much time has passed and yet more than coming closer to resolving these conflicts, which would imply questioning structural problems, what we see today is that conflicts of the same style continue to arise in new places and how managing them remains as nefarious as ever, when not plainly culturalist or racist. At the same time, other conflicts arise, which, at first glance, appear different in form but similar in substance, such as attacks and opposition to juvenile centers.

It is disheartening to see that the underlying problem remains unsolved even after the fifteen years allowed to settle on an effective and sustainable permanent location for the mosque in Premià de Mar. The place of worship is still in the Escola Voramar building. Over the years, it has been maintained and expanded, converting the space and with it the mosque into a civic center of about 1,500 square meters that, apart from serving as oratory, is also expected to host other entities and various activities, while the lot on Joan Prim Street, owned by the Muslim community and where a mosque had been planned fifteen years ago, would be used as an annex to the new civic center.

In this sense, an urgent issue should be pointed out, about which warning was given in the report mentioned above (see SAFI et al. 2021). The Islamophobia exercised by the administrations towards Muslim institutions, due to its appearance of neutrality and as a sign of a structural problem, is undoubtedly the most worrying. Institutional and structural racism are issues that should be addressed with some urgency: they end up legitimizing all other aggressions. Institutional Islamophobia creates precarious and informal conditions that later serve as evidence to blame the marginalized for their condition. In the case of places of worship, it is especially worrying because it complicates integration in similar conditions to the rest of the people in our society. Similar racist and discriminatory narratives and practices can be found in other structural areas such as housing, police, judicial, and labor. We are thinking here of the legal and administrative obstacles that project a certain opacity on the community, which some neighbors interpret as suspicious. For example, the cases of mosques that end up opening in an informal way, mainly due to the slowness of an administration that does not respond satisfactorily to their needs; it is this informality that some neighbors perceive as suspicious (SAFI et al. 2021, 23).

One should remember that Spain is a non-denominational state and is therefore not obliged to provide buildings for religious groups. Nevertheless, the public administration must assist religious organizations when they are searching for space and to protect groups from discrimination; it appears that some administrations find it challenging to fulfill this duty. In the same way, their failure to act in the face of Islamophobia and aggression constitutes one of the most recurrent and worrying forms of racism in Europe currently. Islamophobia exists, like any other manifestation of racism, simultaneously on an interpersonal, institutional and systemic level. To the extent that its expression implies an asymmetric relationship between the aggressor and the object of such aggression, it is the ability to attack and denigrate with impunity that mobilizes most of the actions perceived as Islamophobic (SAFI et al. 2021, 16).

Thus, the individual who naturalizes his rejection of the Muslim religion and those he identifies as its practitioners and channels the phobia as a normal response to people or property, or who, being aware of the moral or legal sanction that his act may call forth, trusts that the administration will be unwilling or unable to take action. Here lies the power that a whole system of representations naturalizes and legitimizes, reinforced by the neglect, indifference or tacit approval of the police and judicial apparatus, and in general by the public administrations called upon to respond to the action in question (SAFI et al. 2021, 16).

Similarly, it is essential to comment on the relationship between abstract and symbolic discourses and individual and institutional actions. For this purpose, it is convenient to refer to the following words of Arun Kundnani, when he explains that Islamophobia is not "is not primarily an expression of hatred or negativity towards Muslims or Islam but a way of connecting people's frustrations, fears, and desires to an explanatory framework that has a fixed idea of 'the Muslim' at its center" (Kundnani 2016, 10). So Islamophobia implies "an ideological displacement of political antagonisms onto the plane of culture, where they can be explained in terms of the fixed nature of the 'Other'" (Kundnani 2016, 7).

Following this line of thought, it is essential to realize that Islamophobia gives meaning to a series of discriminatory and racist actions and constitutes the ideology of what we could call everyday anti-Muslim racism. In other words, intersubjective concrete actions and attacks are often related to other local and institutional factors, which only make sense in a broader discursive and symbolic articulation by virtue of ideas such as the clash of civilizations or cultures. This also means that although the manifestations of Islamophobia seem to be different, any serious analysis must analyze them in relationship to each other. Islamophobia is the wellspring ideology that justifies verbal aggression, violent attacks, institutional deprivation, and community neglect (SAFI et al. 2021, 28).

Abbreviations

AIAT: Islamic Association At-Tauba. Association founded for the management of the premises that would function from then on as a mosque and a madrasa, a Koranic and Arabic school, on Verge de Núria Street in Premià de Mar.

CICC: Consell Islàmic Cultural de Catalunya (Islamic Cultural Council of Catalonia). A federation of Muslim communities established in Catalonia, founded with the purpose of acting as an interlocutor with Catalan institutions.

CiU: Convergència i Unió (Convergence and Union). A Catalan nationalist electoral alliance in that lasted from 1978 to 2015. It was a federation of two constituent parties, the larger Democratic Convergence of Catalonia (CDC), a more traditional liberal center party, and its smaller counterpart, the Democratic Union of Catalonia (UDC), a more conservative Christian democratic party.

CPpC: Coordinadora Premià per la Convivència (Premià for Convivencia Coordinating Committee). An interest group of denizens and entities of Premià de Mar who expressed their concern about the continual erosion of social harmony and peace in the town. The participants rejected the xenophobic attitudes of the neighbors opposed to the construction of the mosque and criticized the actions of the town council.

ERC: Esquerra Repúblicana de Catalunya (Republican Left of Catalonia). A Catalan pro-independence social-democratic political party.

ICV: Iniciativa per Catalunya Verds (Initiative for Catalonia Greens). An eco-socialist political party that lasted from 1987 to 2019.

PNM-JP: Plataforma "No a la Mesquita en la Calle Joan Prim" (Platform "No to the Mosque on Joan Prim Street").

PSC: Partit dels Socialistes de Catalunya (Socialists' Party of Catalonia). A social-democratic political party and the Catalan branch of the Spanish Socialist Workers' Party (PSOE).

PxC: Plataforma per Catalunya (Platform for Catalonia). A far-right political party which centered its political agenda around controlling immigration and its opposition to Catalan independence. It was strongly anti-Islamic, and was widely considered a racist, xenophobic far-right political force. It lasted from 2002 to 2019 where it merged with VOX, a Spanish nationalist right-wing party.

PxP: Plataforma per Premià de Mar (Platform for Premià de Mar). A local branch of Platform for Catalonia.

Chronology

Table A.1

DATE	SCALE	EVENT
1987	Town	First official Ramadan held in Premià de Mar.
1988	Town Hall/Building	Permission granted for the oratory on Verge de Núria St.
1993	Building "Gray Blocks"	First complaints by some of the neighbors in the building.
1995	Town Hall/Building	Municipal technical inspection of the premises.
November 1996	Town Hall/Building	Permissions revoked.
December 1996	Building	Meeting between the neighbors-owners of flats in the building dealing with the "foreign" neighbors-renters and the mosque.
February 1997	Town Hall/Building	The oratory was ordered to be closed. Redevelopment work on the premise began.
March 1997	AIAT	AIAT buys a plot in Joan Prim St.
June, 1997	Town	Special Plan for the building of a school and a mosque in Joan Prim St endorsed by the College of Architects of Catalonia.
June 1997	Neighborhood: Maresme/Building	First neighborhood mobilizations against the new construction.
October 1997	Town Hall/Building	Special Plan approved by the Town Council.
July 1999	Ca n'Anglada (Terrassa)	Racist attacks on Moroccans, mosques and establishments run by Moroccans in the Ca n'Anglada neighborhood in the city of Terrassa (Catalonia).

DATE	SCALE	EVENT
January 2000	Neighborhood/Town/ Region	Demonstration against insecurity and migrants. Clashes between fascists and anti-fascists.
February 2000	El Ejido (Andalusia)	Racist attacks in El Ejido (Andalusia) on Moroccans, their shacks, and establishments run by Moroccans.
December 2000	Catalonia/Town/ Building	Confirmation of the order to close the premises in Verge de Núria St.
April 2001	Town/Neighborhood: Barri Cotet	Proposal to use premises (50 m²) in Barri Cotet. Rejected by residents and AIAT.
April 2001	Town Hall/AIAT	Sit-in at the premises in Verge de Núria to find an alternative location for the celebration of Ramadan.
July 2001	Town Hall/AIAT	Permissions for the construction and activity licenses requested by AIAT.
September 2001	Global	Terrorist attacks at the twin towers in New York City.
October 2001	Town Hall/AIAT	The premises in Verge de Núria was ordered closed. Instead, AIAT was offered the old school premises of Escola Voramar as a temporary location for their activities.
November 2001	Town	5,554 signatures delivered to the Town Hall requesting that the Town Council deny the construction permit for a mosque in Joan Prim St.
December 2001	Town Hall/Town	A new location was proposed in the Barri Banyeres.
January 2002	Town Hall/ Neighborhood: Barri Banyeres	An agreement was reached with the owners of the land in the Barri Banyeres neighborhood.
February 2002	Neighborhoods: Barri Banyeres/Maresme	1,500 signatures were handed in against the building in Barri Banyeres.
April 2002	AIAT	AIAT declines the proposal in Barri Banyeres and reclaims their right to build in Joan Prim St.
April 12, 2002	Town Hall/AIAT	The Town Council announced their intention to evict AIAT from the Escola Voramar in 48 hours.
April 18, 2002	Neighborhood: Barri Banyeres	A roadblock to protest the decision to allow the mosque in Barri Banyeres.
April 19, 2002	Town Hall/AIAT	The mayor announced the grant of the building license per "legal imposition."

April 19, 2002	Town/ Neighborhood/AIAT	Prayer in the premises of Joan Prim Street and a "noisy rally" by some neighbors.
April 23, 2002	Town	Demonstration in the town square and reading of the "Manifesto for the Respect of Civil Rights" signed by the Coordinadora Premià per la Convivència (CPpC).
April 27, 2002	Town	Declaration for Convivencia in Premià de Mar signed and presented by all the municipal political parties.
May 2, 2002	Town	Rally held by CPpC gathering around 300 people and reading of the Manifesto for the Respect of Civil Rights.
May 12, 2002	Town	A demonstration organized by CPpC marched through the streets of Premià in favor of *convivencia* and against intolerance and racism. About 1,000 people gathered and 30 local and state organizations joined in, including unions and NGOs.
May 18, 2002	Town	A demonstration led by Plataforma per Catalunya took place in Premià de Mar, gathering between 1,000 and 1,500 people against the building of the mosque. It ended with a clash between fascists and anti-fascists.
September 5, 2002	Town	An agreement and the Pact for a New Citizenship was signed by the town council and AIAT. Later Premià de Mar, El Masnou, Mataró and Pineda de Mar signed a collaboration agreement with the Generalitat de Catalunya for the implementation of a Regional Immigration Plan, and the Municipal Council for Coexistence was constituted as a body that would work on proposals and projects related to immigration in the town.

Bibliography

Agamben, Giorgio. 1995. *Homo Sacer. El Poder Soberano y la Nuda Vida*. Valencia: Pre-textos.

———. 2010. *Signatura Rerum. Sobre el Método*. Barcelona: Anagrama.

Agrela Romero, Belén. 2006. "Análisis Antropológico de las Políticas Sociales Dirigidas a la Población Inmigrante." PhD diss., University of Granada.

Aixelà Cabré, Yolanda. 2007. "Muslims in Spain. The case of Maghrebins in Alicante." *Journal for the Study of Religions and Ideologies*, no.17, 84–100.

Álvarez, Ignasi. 2002. "La Construcción del Inintegrable Cultural." In *Inmigrantes: ¿Cómo los Tenemos?* edited by J. de Lucas and F. Torres. Madrid: Talasa.

Anderson, Benedict. 1993. *Comunidades Imaginadas. Reflexiones Sobre el Origen y la Difusión del Nacionalismo*. México DF: Fondo de Cultura Económica.

Ansola, Emma. 2001. "La comunitat musulmana de Premià de Mar acata l'ordre de tancament de la mesquita." *El Punt*, November 13, 2001.

———. 2002a. "Veïns del voltant del polígon de Premià recullen 700 signatures contra la mesquita." *El Punt*, February 1, 2002.

———. 2002b. "Una escletxa en el conflicte per la mesquita." *El Punt*, April 25, 2002.

———. 2002c. "Aproven el reglament del Consell Municipal per a la Convivència de Premià de Mar." *Vilaweb*, September 18, 2002.

———. 2003. "El govern de Premià de Mar vol fer canvis en el Consell de la Convivència i atura les reunions de treball." *Vilaweb*, October 14, 2003.

Appadurai, Arjun. 1996. *Modernity at Large: Cultural Dimensions of Globalization*. Minneapolis: University of Minnesota Press.

Aranda, Alberto and Guillermo Cruz, dirs. 2005. *¡Mezquita No!* Barcelona: A Contraluz Films/tururut art infogràfic. Documentary film.

Arenós, Paloma and Antonia de la Fuente. 2001. "El Ayuntamiento de Premià de Mar cede un edificio para una mezquita musulmana." *La Vanguardia*, March 27, 2001.

Ariño, Gerard. 2010. "La tensió social que va viure Premià de Mar amb la crisi de la mesquita el 2002 s'ha refredat, però el debat encara no està tancat." *El Punt / Hoy +*, February 8, 2010.

Aramburu Otazu, Mikel. 2002. *Los Otros y Nosotros. Imágenes del Inmigrante en Ciutat Vella de Barcelona*. Madrid: Ministerio de Educación, Cultura y Deporte.

Astor, Astor. 2009. "'¡Mezquita No!': The Origins of Mosque Opposition in Spain." *GRITIM-UPF Working Paper Series*, no. 3, 1–42.

Azurmendi, Mikel. 2001. *Estampas de El Ejido*. Madrid: Taurus.

———. 2002. "Inmigrar para vivir en democracia." *El País*, January 20, 2002.

Bacchi, Carol. 2009. *Analysing Policy: What's the Problem Represented to Be?* Frenchs Forest: Pearson Education.

———. 2010. "Poststructuralism, Discourse and Problematization: Implications for Gender Mainstreaming." *Kvinder, Køn & Forskning*, no. 4, 62–72.

Balaguer, Victor. 1985. *Guia de Barcelona á Arenys de Mar por el Ferro-carril.* Barcelona: Jaime Jepús y Ramon Villegas.

Balibar, Étienne. 1991. "Is There a 'Neo-Racism'?" In *Race, Nation, Class. Ambigous Identities*, edited by Étienne Balibar and Immanuel Wallerstein. London: Verso.

Banco Mundial. 1962. *Informe del Banco Internacional de Reconstrucción y Fomento. El Desarrollo Económico de España.* Madrid: Oficina de Coordinación y Planificación Económica.

Batet, Estel. 2001. "L'Ajuntament de Premià de Mar proposa instal·lar la mesquita al polígon industrial." *Hoy*, December 6, 2001.

Batet, Estel. 2002. "El disseny de la mesquita de Premià es negociarà amb els veïns." *Avui*, June 3, 2002.

Beck, Ulrich. 1999. *What Is Globalization?* Cambridge: Polity Press.

Berlanga, E. 2002. "Los musulmanes de Premià de Mar denunciarán al Ayuntamiento." *ABC*, April 23, 2002.

Bernabé, Mònica. 2001. "Els musulmans de Premià de Mar accepten traslladar la mesquita al polígon, però amb condicions." *El Punt*, December 11, 2001.

Bernabé, Mònica, and Oriol Ribet. 2001. "Més de cinc mil persones rebutgen la construcció d'una mesquita a Premià de Mar." *El Punt*, November 26, 2001.

Bosch, Mariano, M. Ángeles Carnero, and Lídia Farré. 2015. "Rental housing discrimination and the persistence of ethnic enclaves." *Working Papers*. Serie AD 2011-10, Instituto Valenciano de Investigaciones Económicas, S.A. (Ivie).

Bourdieu, Pierre. 1999. *Contrafuegos: Reflexiones para Servir a la Resistencia Contra la Invasión Neoliberal.* Barcelona: Anagram.

———. 2003. "Participant Objectivation." *The Journal of the Royal Anthropological Institute* 9, no. 2: 281–294.

———. 2007. *El sentido practico.* Madrid: Siglo Veintiuno Editores.

Bourgois, Philippe. 2002. *In Search of Respect: Selling Crack in el Barrio.* Cambridge: Cambridge University Press.

Bravo López, Fernando. 2012. *En Casa Ajena. Bases Intelectuales del Antisemitismo y la Islamofobia.* Barcelona: Edicions Bellaterra.

Brenner, Neil, and Nik Theodore. 2002. "Cities and the Geographies of Actually Existing Neoliberalism." *Antipode* 34, no. 3, 349–379.

Broll. 2020. *The key could be a name. Finding evidence of discrimination in access to the rental housing market in Barcelona.* Barcelona: Barcelona City Council. https://ajuntament.barcelona.cat/dretsidiversitat/sites/default/files/THE_KEY_COULD_BE_A_NAME.pdf.

Burawoy, Michael. 1998. "The Extended Case Method." *Sociological Theory*, 16, no.1.

———. 2000. "Introduction: Reaching for the Global." In *Global Ethnography: Forces, Connections, and Imaginations in a Postmodern World*, edited by Michael Burawoy. Berkeley: University of California Press.

Cañizares, María Jesús. 2002. "Historia de una mezquita." *ABC*, May 26, 2002.

Carles, Montse. 2000. "La violencia juvenil por el conflicto racial de Premià se salda con tres heridos." *El País*, January 29, 2000.

Castells, Manuel. 1973. *Movimientos Sociales Urbanos.* Madrid: Siglo Veintiuno Editores.

Cedó Garcia, Fede. 2002a. "Los vecinos de Premià vuelven a recoger firmas contra la mezquita." *El Mundo*, February 6, 2002.

———. 2002b. "Premià levantará una mezquita en Can Banyeres pese a las críticas." *El Mundo*, February 26, 2002.

Cedó Garcia, Fede. 2002c. "La ultraderecha, con los 'antimezquita' de Premià." *El Mundo*, April 29, 2002.

Cesari, Jocelyne. 2005. "Mosque Conflicts in European Cities: Introduction." *Journal of Ethnic and Migration Studies* 31, no.6, 1015–1024.

———. 2006. *Securitization and Religious Divides in Europe. Muslims In Western Europe After 9/11: Why the Term Islamophobia is More a Predicament Than an Explanation.* Submission to the Changing Landscape of Citizenship and Security 6th PCRD of the European Commission.

Coll i Monteagudo, Ramon. 2009. *Història Pintoresca de Premià de Mar.* Premià de Mar: Clavell Cultura.

Debord, Guy. 1995. *La Sociedad del Espectáculo.* Buenos Aires: La Marca.

Delgado, Manuel. 1997. "Introducció: Qui pot ser immigrant a la ciutat?" In *Ciutat i immigració. Urbanitats*, edited by M. Delagdo. Barcelona: CCCB.

———. 1999. *El Animal Público: Hacia una Antropología de los Espacios Urbanos.* Barcelona: Anagrama.

———. 2006. "Nuevas Retóricas para la Exclusión Social." In *Flujos Migratorios y su (des)control. Puntos de Vista Pluridisciplinarios*, edited by R. Bergalli. Barcelona: Anthropos.

Douglas, Mary. 1966. *Purity and Danger: An Analysis of Concepts of Pollution and Taboo.* London: Routledge.

Editorial Office, *ABC*. 2002. "El Ayuntamiento de Premià ya ha dado el visto bueno a la mezquita." *ABC*, May 19, 2002.

Editorial Office, *La Razón*. 2001. "Clausuran una mezquita en Premià tras un pacto vecinal." *La Razón*, November 13, 2001.

———. 2002. "Premià crea el Consejo para la Convivencia tras la polémica de la nueva mezquita." *La Razón*, September 18, 2002.

Editorial Office, *La Vanguardia*. 1999. "El Parlament expresa su 'enérgico rechazo' a los actos racistes." *La Vanguardia*, July 29, 1999.

———. 2002. "Mas afirma que ya propuso, antes que Carod, la expulsión de imanes 'radicales.'" *La Vanguardia*, May 23, 2002.

ERC Premià de Mar. 2021. "Posem en marxa als regidors i regidores de barri" *ERC Premià de Mar.* Retrieved from https://locals.esquerra.cat/premiademar/article /106738/regidors-i-regidores-de-barri March 10, 2021.

Espada, Arcadi, and Sílvia Marimon. 2003. "Olvidar Ca n'Anglada." El País, May 15, 2003.

Foucault, Michel. 1969. *La Arqueología del Saber.* Madrid: Siglo XXI.

————. 2006. *Las Palabras y las Cosas. Una Arqueología de las Ciencias Humanes.* Madrid: Siglo Veintiuno Editores.

Franquesa, Jaume. 2005. "Sa Calatrava mon Amour. Etnografía d'un Barri Atrapat en la Geografia del Capital." PhD diss., University of Barcelona.

Franquesa, Jaume. 2007. "Vaciar y Llenar, o la Lógica Espacial de la Neoliberalización." *Revista Español de Investigaciones Sociológicas,* no. 118, 123–150.

de la Fuente, Antonia. 2001a. "Premià retira el local municipal prometido para la mezquita ante la presión vecinal." *La Vanguardia,* April 11, 2001.

————. 2001b. "Oposición a que los musulmanes alcen una mezquita en su solar." *La Vanguardia,* July 6, 2001.

————. 2001c. "El Ayuntamiento de Premià cierra la mezquita de la calle Verge de Núria." *La Vanguardia,* November 11, 2001.

————. 2002. "El rezo de unos musulmanes en su propio solar irrita a unos vecinos de Premià." *La Vanguardia,* April 20, 2002.

Gabinet d'Estudis Socials, Centro de Referencia en España, Observatorio Europeo contra el Racismo y la Xenofobia (EUMC). 2002. "Estudio del conflicto de la mezquita de Premiá de Mar." Barcelona.

Gale, Richard. 2005. "Representing the City: Mosques and the Planning Process in Birmingham." *Journal of Ethnic and Migration Studies* 31, no. 6, 1161–1179.

de Galembert, Claire. 2005. "The City's 'Nod of Approval' for the Mantes-la-Jolie Mosque Project: Mistaken Traces of Recognition." *Journal of Ethnic and Migration Studies* 31, no. 6, 1141–1159.

Gil Araujo, Sandra. 2010. *Las Argucias de la Integración: Políticas Migratorias, Construcción Nacional y Cuestión Social.* Madrid: Iepala.

Gluckman, Max. 1958. "Analysis of a Social Situation in Modern Zululand." *Rhodes-Livingstone Papers,* 28.

————. 2008. "Ethnographic Data in British Social Anthropology." In *The Manchester School. Practice and Ethnographic Praxis in Anthropology,* edited by T. M. S. Evens and Don Handelman. Oxford: Berghahn Books.

Guillaumin, Colette. 1972. *L'Idéologie Raciste, Genèse et Langage Actuel.* Paris/The Hague: Mouton.

Gupta, Akhil, and James Ferguson. 1997. "Culture, Power, Place: Ethnography at the End of an Era." In *Culture, Power, Place: Explorations in Critical Anthropology,* edited by Akhil Gupta and James Ferguson. Durham: Duke University Press.

Guri, Ferran. 2003. "Evolució Urbana de Premià de Mar." Unedited text in the collection of Els Estudis d'Enginyeria Tècnica d'Obres Publiques.

Haider, Asad. 2018. *Mistaken Identity: Race and Class in the Age of Trump.* London: Verso.

Halliday, Fred. 1999. "'Islamophobia' Reconsidered." *Ethnic and Racial Studies* 22, no. 5, 892–902.

Hannerz, Ulf. 1998. "Transnational Research." In *Handbook of Methods in Cultural Anthropology,* edited by H.R. Bernard. London: AltaMira Press.

Harvey, David. 1990. *The Condition of Postmodernity.* Cambridge: Blackwell.

————. 2001. *Spaces of Capital: Towards a Critical Geography.* Edinburgh: Edinburgh University Press.

IDESCAT 2010. Statiscal Institute of Catalonia. https://www.idescat.cat/?lang=en.

Jabardo Velasco, Mercedes. 1999. "Migración Clandestina y Agricultura Intensiva: la Reestructuración del Mercado de Trabajo en el Maresme Catalán." In *Inmigrantes entre nosotros: trabajo, cultura y educación intercultural*, edited by Encarna Soriano and Francisco Checa y Olmos. Barcelona: Icaria.

Jonker, Gerdien. 2005. "The Mevlana Mosque in Berlin-Kreuzberg: An Unsolved Conflict." *Journal of Ethnic and Migration Studies* 31, no. 6, 1067–1081.

Juanola, Laura. 1997. "Un grup de veïns vol expulsar d'un bloc de pisos de Premià trenta famílies africanes." *El Punt*, January 21, 1997.

———. 2001. "Els musulmans demanen permís a l'Ajuntament per construir la mesquita de Premià de Mar." *El Punt*, July 06, 2001.

J.V. 2002. "Premià constituye un consejo para la convivencia." *El País*, September 16, 2002.

Kapferer, Bruce. 2005. "Situations, Crisis, and the Anthropology of the Concrete. The Contributions of Max Gluckman." *Social Analysis* 49, no. 3, 85–122.

Kumar, Deepa. 2012. *Islamophobia: The Cultural Logic of Empire.* New York: Haymarket.

Kundnani, Arun. 2016. "Islamophobia: Lay Ideology of US-led Empire." Accessed December 30, 2021. https://www.kundnani.org/wp-content/uploads/Kundnani-Islamophobia-as-lay-ideology-of-US-empire.pdf

Kymlicka, Will. 1995. *Multicultural Citizenship: A Liberal Theory of Minority Rights.* Oxford: Oxford University Press.

Landman, Nico and Wendy Wessels. 2005. "The Visibility of Mosques in Dutch Towns." *Journal of Ethnic and Migration Studies* 31, no. 6, 1125–1140.

Lean, Nathan. 2012. *The Islamophobia Industry: How the Right Manufactures Hatred of Muslims.* London: Verso.

Lefebvre, Henri. 1976. *Espacio y Política: El Derecho a la Ciudad II.* Barcelona: Península.

———i. 1991. *The Production of Space.* Oxford: Blackwell.

López Bargados, Alberto. 2009. "Narrativas del Miedo: Sobre la Construcción de la Amenaza Islamista en Barcelona." In *Rastros de Dixan. Islamofobia y Construcción del Enemigo en la Era post 11-S*, edited by Abdennur Prado, Alberto Martínez, Alberto López Bargados, Benet Salellas Vilar, David Fernández and Iñaki Rivera Beiras, 111–140. Barcelona: Virus Editorial.

López Sánchez, Pere. 1986. *El Centro Histórico: Un Lugar para el Conflicto.* Barcelona: Geo Crítica: Edicions de la Universitat de Barcelona.

Lundsteen, Martin. 2015. "Conflicts and Convivencia: An Ethnography of the Social Effects of 'The Crisis' in a Small Catalan Town." PhD diss., Universitat de Barcelona.

———. 2018. "'El Moro'—Discovering the Hidden Coloniality of the Contemporary Spanish/Catalan Society and its Colonial Subjects." In *Postcolonial Europe: Comparative Reflections after the Empires*, edited by Lars Jensen, Júlia Suárez Krabbe, Christian Groes-Green and Zoran L. Pecic. New York: Rowman and Littlefield.

———. 2022. *Convivencia: Migration and Urban Transformation in a Small Catalan Town.* Challenging Migration Studies Series. New York and London: Rowman and Littlefield International.

Lundsteen, Martin and Mostafà Shaimi. 2010. In revision. "Islamophobia, Anti-Muslim Racism and Capitalism." In *Historical Materialism.*

Majoral, Roser, Francisco López Palomeque, and Jaume Font. 2002. *Cataluña. Un Análisis Territorial.* Barcelona: Ariel Geografía.

Mamdani, Mahmood. 2004. *Good Muslim, Bad Muslim: America, the Cold War, and the Roots of Terror.* New York: Three Leaves Press, Doubleday.

Mancera, Eva. 2001a. "5.500 firmes s'oposen a una mesquita a Premià." *El Periódico,* July 06, 2001.

———. 2001b. "Premià de Mar presenta 5.5554 firmes contra una mesquita." *El Periódico,* November 27, 2001.

Manço, Ural and Meryem Kanmaz. 2005. "From Conflict to Co-operation Between Muslims and Local Authorities in a Brussels Borough: Schaerbeek." *Journal of Ethnic and Migration Studies* 31, no. 6, 1105–1123.

Maresme County Council. 2003. *Estudi Prospectiu d'immigració a la comarca del Maresme.*

Martín Corrales, Eloy. 2002. *La Imagen del Magrebí en España: Una Perspectiva Histórica, Siglos XVI-XX.* Barcelona: Bellaterra.

Martínez Soler, Montserrat, and Ajuntament de Terrassa. 2008. *Monogràfic: El Pla de Barris: Ca n'Anglada, Torre-Sana, Vilardell i Montserrat. 2005–2008.* Terrassa: Informe de Conjuntura de Terrassa.

Martínez Veiga, Ubaldo. 1991. "Organización y Percepción del Espacio: El Espacio Urbano." In *Antropología de los Pueblos de España,* edited by Joan Prat, Ubaldo Martínez Veiga, Jesús Contreras and Isidoro Moreno. Madrid: Taurus.

———. 1999. *Pobreza, Segregación y Exclusión Espacial: La Vivienda de los Inmigrantes Extranjeros en España.* Barcelona: Icaria.

———. 2001. *El Ejido: Discriminación, Exclusión Social y Racismo.* Madrid: Catarata.

Marx, Karl. 2008. *El Capital,* vol. 1. Barcelona: Edicions 62/Diputació de Barcelona.

Mateo Dieste, Josep-Lluís. 1997. *El "Moro" entre los Primitivos: El Caso del Protectorado Español en Marruecos.* Barcelona: Fundación La Caixa.

McLoughlin, Seán. 2005. "Mosques and the Public Space: Conflict and Cooperation in Bradford." *Journal of Ethnic and Migration Studies* 31, no. 6, 1045–1066.

Miles, Robert, and Malcom Brown. 2003. *Racism.* London: Routledge.

Mingione, Enzo. 1981. *Social conflict and the City.* Glasgow: Basil Blackwell.

Mintz, Sidney. 1998. "The Localization of Anthropological Practice. From Area Studies to Transnationalism." *Critique of Anthropology* 18, no. 2, 117–133.

Mitchell, Clyde. 2008. "Case and Situation Analysis." In *The Manchester School. Practice and Ethnographic Praxis in Anthropology,* edited by T. M. S. Evens and D. Handelman. Oxford: Berghahn Books.

Monnet, Nadja. 2002. *La Formación del Espacio Público: Una Mirada Etnológica sobre el Casc Antic de Barcelona.* Madrid: Catarata.

Moreras, Jordi. 2004. "Conflictos en Cataluña." In *Atlas de la Inmigración Marroquí en España*, edited by Bernabé López García and Mohammed Berriane. Madrid: Taller de Estudios Internacionales Mediterráneos, UAM, OPI, Secretaría de Estado de Inmigración y emigración, Ministerio de Trabajo y Asuntos Sociales.

Moreras, Jordi. 2009. *Una Mesquita al Barri. Conflicte, Espai Públic i Inserció Urbana dels Oratoris Musulmans a Catalunya*. Barcelona: Fundació Bofill.

Müller-Uri, Fanny, and Benjamin Opratko. 2016. "Islamophobia as Anti-Muslim Racism: Racism without 'Races,' Racism without Racists." *Islamophobia Studies Journal* 3, no.2, 116–129.

Narotzky, Susana. 2005. "The Production of Knowledge and the Production of Hegemony: Anthropological Theory and Political Struggles in Spain." *Journal of the World Anthropology Network*, no. 1, 35–54.

Oñate, Sandra. 2002. "Segueix la polémica per la mesquita de Premià." *El Periódico*, April 19, 2002.

Oró Badia, Antoni. 2004. *Interculturalitat*. Unpublished work for MA. Premià de Mar.

de Orovio, Nacho. 1999. "Hemos contenido a los que pedían respuesta." *La Vanguardia*, July 18, 1999.

de Orovio, Nacho and Francesca Rodríguez. 1999. "Dos manifestaciones contra el racismo reúnen a 5.000 personas." *La Vanguardia*, July 28, 1999.

Palou, Ricard. 2001. "Els musulmans de Premià reben el suport dels de tot l'Estat en l'afer de la mesquita." *El Punt*, April 18, 2001.

Palou, Ricard and Iolanda Tarramera. 2001. "El govern de Premià de Mar no tancarà la mesquita perquè ara diu que no té competències per fer-ho." *El Punt*, April 19, 2001.

Pascual i Saüc, Jordi. 2008. "Diversitat Religiosa i Convivència Intercultural. O com Començar a Perdre la por a les Mesquites." In *Diversitat Cultural i Globalització: Nous Reptes per al Moviment Associatiu*, edited by Jordi Pascual i Saüc and Elena Rovira. Barcelona: Fundación Desenvolupament Comunitari. Ajuntament de Barcelona.

Pascual i Saüc, Jordi and Jonatan Sánchez Rico. 2005. *La Convivència Intercultural a Premià de Mar. Diagnòstic després del Conflicte de la Mesquita*. Barcelona: Informe elaborat per l'AEP Desenvolupament Comunitari.

Pelàez, Lluc. 2002. "Premià de Mar, un (mal) Ejemplo de Movilización Ciudadana." Accessed December 30, 2021. http://fundacionbetiko.org/wp-content/uploads/2012/11/premia-de-mar-un-mal-ejemplo-de-movilizacion-ciudadana.pdf

Pérez, Mercè. 2001. "Premià de Mar recoge 5.500 firmas contra la instalación de una mezquita." *El País*, November 27, 2001.

———. 2002a. "Los musulmanes de Premià acondicionan un solar para rezar al aire libre." *El País*, April 18, 2002.

———. 2002b. "Autorizada una mezquita en Premià mientras se radicalizan las protestas." *El País*, April 27, 2002.

———. 2002 "El Ayuntamiento de Premiá autoriza una mezquita 'por imperativo legal.'" *El País*, April 27, 2002.

Pétonnet, Colette. 1982. "L'Observation flottante. L'exemple d'un Cimetière Parisien." *L'Homme* 22, no. 4, 37–47.

Polanyi, Karl. 2001. *The Great Transformation. The Political and Economic Origin of our Time.* Boston: Beacon Press.

Prado, Abdennur. 2008. *El Retorn de l'Islam a Catalunya.* Barcelona: Llibres de l'índex.

———. 2009. "La Islamofobia como Ideología Dominante." In *Rastros de Dixan. Islamofobia y Construcción del Enemigo en la Era post 11-S,* edited by Abdennur Prado, Alberto Martínez, Alberto López Bargados, Benet Salellas Vilar, David Fernández and Iñaki Rivera Beiras, 37–64. Barcelona: Virus Editorial.

Prado, Carlos G. 2000. *Starting with Foucault: An Introduction to Genealogy.* Oxford: Westview Press.

Premià de Mar City Council. 2002. *Pacte per la nova ciutadania a Premià de Mar.*

———. 1997. The Special Plan for the Development of Community Buildings.

Prytherch, David. 2001. "El Paisaje Ideológico: La Huerta, la Globalización y la Modernidad Valenciana. Una Mirada Norteamericana." *Metode,* no. 31. Accessed December 30, 2021. https://metode.es/revistas-metode/monograficos/el-paisaje -ideologico-la-huerta-la-globalizacion-y-la-modernidad-valenciana-una-mirada -norteamericana.html

PSC, CiU, PP, ERC and IC-V de Premià de Mar. 2002. "Declaració per la convivència a Premià de Mar." *El Punt,* April 27, 2002.

Punch, Michael. 2005. "Problem Drug Use and the Political Economy of Urban Restructuring: Heroin, Class and Governance in Dublin." *Antipode,* no. 37, 754–774.

Reeves, Frank, Tahir Abbas, and Dulce Pedroso. 2009. "The 'Dudley Mosque Project': a Case of Islamophobia and Local Politics." *The Political Quarterly,* no. 80, 502–516.

Ribet, Oriol. 2002a. "Demà, pregàries al carrer Joan Prim." *El Punt,* April 18, 2002.

———. 2002b. "La reposta dels musulmans." *El Punt,* April 19, 2002.

Rincón, Reyes. 2008. "La mezquita de Sevilla se queda otra vez sin suelo por un error municipal." El País, October 17, 2008.

Robertson, Roland. 1992. *Globalization: Social Theory and Global Culture.* London: Sage.

Robinson, Cedric J. 2000. *Black Marxism: The Making of the Black Radical Tradition.* Chapel Hill, NC: The University of North Carolina Press.

Rodríguez, Francesca. 1999a. "Una batalla campal entre jóvenes acaba en ataques de tinte racista." *La Vanguardia,* July 14, 1999.

———. 1999b. "Erupción racista." *La Vanguardia,* July 15, 1999.

———. 1999c. "Los magrebíes evitan salir de casa tras cinco días de violenca racista." *La Vanguardia,* July 16, 1999.

———. 1999d. "Primeras detenciones." *La Vanguardia,* July 17, 1999.

———. 1999e. "Once detenidos por los últimos enfrentamientos en Ca n'Anglada." *La Vanguardia,* July 19, 1999.

———. 2000. "Terrassa invierte en Ca n'Anglada para evitar su marginación." *La Vanguardia,* January 15, 2000.

Rosón Lorente, Francisco Javier. 2005. "Tariq's return? Muslimophobia, Muslimophilia and the Formation of Ethnicised Religious Communities in Southern Spain." *Migration: A European Journal of International Migration and Ethnic Relations,* nos. 43–45, 87–95.

SAFI, Martin Lundsteen, and Alberto López Bargados. 2021. *Fent Visible allò Invisible. Informe Anual de l'Observatori de la Islamofòbia a Catalunya 2020.* Barcelona: SAFI.

Saint-Blancat, Chantal, and Ottavia Schmidt di Friedberg. 2005. "Why Are Mosques a Problem? Local Politics and Fear of Islam in Northern Italy." *Journal of Ethnic and Migration Studies* 31, no. 6: 1083–1104.

Sánchez, Raúl, and Analía Plaza. 2021. "El mapa de las alturas de todos los edificios de España: busca tu barrio." *El Diario*, September 29, 2021.

Santamaría, Enrique. 2002. *La Incógnita del Extraño. Una Aproximación a la Significación Sociológica de la 'Inmigración no Comunitaria.'* Rubí: Anthropos Editorial.

Schumpeter, Joseph A. 1994. *Capitalism, Socialism and Democracy.* London: Taylor and Francis Ltd.

Sennett, Richard. 2006. *The Culture of the New Capitalism.* London: Yale University Press.

Smith, Neil. 1993. "Homeless/Global: Scaling Places." In *Mapping the Futures: Local Cultures, Global Change*, edited by J. Bird. London: Routledge.

Stolcke, Verena. 1995. "Talking Culture: New Boundaries, New Rhetorics of Exclusion in Europe." *Current Anthropology* 36, no. 1, 1–24.

Taguieff, Pierre-André. 1995. "Las Metamorfosis Ideológicas del Racismo y la Crisis del Antirracismo." In *Racismo, Antirracismo e Inmigración*, edited by Juan Pedro Alvite. San Sebastian: Gakoa.

Tarramera, Iolanda. 2001. "Els musulmans de Premià de Mar traslladen la mesquita en un local del barri Cotet." *El Punt*, April 01, 2001.

The Cartographic and Geological Institute of Catalonia. 2010a. "Map of the Locations." http://www.icc.cat/vissir3/

———. 2010b. "Premià within the Maresme Region and near Barcelona." http://www.icc.cat/vissir3/

———. 2010c. "Urban Actions." http://www.icc.cat/vissir3/

Tria, Jordi. 2003. "Escolarització, Cultura i Societat. Exploració Comparada a Premià de Mar i Sabadell." PhD diss., Universitat Autònoma de Barcelona.

Tsing, Anna. 2000. "The Global Situation." *Cultural Anthropology* 15, no. 3, 327–360.

Vaccaro, Ismael, and Oriol Bertrán. 2007. "Consuming space, nature and culture: patrimonial discussions in the hyper-modern era." *Tourism Geographies* 9, no. 3, 254-274.

Wacquant, Loïc. 2007. *Los Condenados de la Ciudad. Gueto, Periferias y Estado.* Madrid: Siglo XXI Editores.

Wallerstein, Immanuel. 1974. *The Modern World-System: Capitalist Agriculture and the Origins of the European World-Economy in the Sixteenth Century*, vol. 1. London: Academic Press.

Weber, Rachel. 2002. "Extracting Value from the City: Neoliberalism and Urban Redevelopment." *Antipode* 34, no. 3, 519–540.

Werbner, Richard P. 1984. "The Manchester School in South-Central Africa." *Annual Review of Anthropology*, no. 13, 157–185.

Wetherell, Margaret, and Jonathan Potter. 1992. *Mapping the Language of Racism. Discourse and the Legitimation of Exploitation.* New York: Columbia University Press.

Wolf, Eric. 1990. *Europe and the People without History*. London: University of California Press.

Zapata-Barrero, Ricard. 2003. "La Ciudadanía en Contextos de Multiculturalidad: Procesos de Cambios de Paradigmas." *Anales de la Cátedra Francisco Suárez,* no. 37, 173–199

Zino Torrazza, Julio. 2006. "Inmigración y Prácticas Sociales Discriminatorias." In *Flujos Migratorios y su (des)control. Puntos de Vista Pluridisciplinarios*, edited by Roberto Bergalli. Barcelona: Anthropos.

Index

About the Author

Martin Lundsteen (MA and PhD in anthropology, University of Barcelona) is Carlsberg Foundation Visiting Fellow at the Centre for Criminology, University of Oxford, and teacher at the University of Barcelona and University of Girona. Currently he is working on the project *Contested Belongings: Emerging Bordering Practices in the EU*. A research project which studies the societal effects of so-called *bordering practices*, that is, how social boundaries are being constituted and enforced through housing in Denmark and Catalonia. Apart from being a member and director of the Observatory of the Anthropology of Urban Conflict (OACU), he is also member of the Research Group on Reciprocity (GER) and the Association Stop Islamophobia (SAFI). His main research interests include political and economic anthropology, informal economy, urban anthropology, mobility, the political management of the poor, Islamophobia and racism. He is the author of the book *Convivencia: Urban Space and Migration in a Small Catalan Town* (Rowman and Littlefield, 2022), and several peer-reviewed articles in journals such as *Journal of Muslims in Europe*, *Dialectical Anthropology*, *Social Anthropology* and *Critical Criminology*, and is publishing a Special Issue on Urban Bordering with *European Urban and Regional Studies*.

www.ingramcontent.com/pod-product-compliance
Lightning Source LLC
Chambersburg PA
CBHW031138270326
41929CB00011B/1677